WHAT WORKS

TARA McMULLIN

WHAT WORKS

A COMPREHENSIVE FRAMEWORK TO CHANGE THE WAY WE APPROACH GOAL SETTING

Published by John Wiley & Sons, Inc., Hoboken, New Jersey.
Published simultaneously in Canada.

For general information on our other products and services or for technical support, please contact our Customer Care Department within the United States at (800) 762-2974, outside the United States at (317) 572-3993 or fax (317) 572-4002.

Wiley publishes in a variety of print and electronic formats and by print-on-demand. Some material included with standard print versions of this book may not be included in e-books or in print-on-demand. If this book refers to media such as a CD or DVD that is not included in the version you purchased, you may download this material at http://booksupport.wiley.com. For more information about Wiley products, visit www.wiley.com.

Library of Congress Cataloging-in-Publication Data

Names: McMullin, Tara, author.
Title: What works : a comprehensive framework to change the way we approach
   goal setting / Tara McMullin.
Description: Hoboken, New Jersey : Wiley, [2023] | Includes index.
Identifiers: LCCN 2022026335 (print) | LCCN 2022026336 (ebook) | ISBN
   9781119906070 (hardback) | ISBN 9781119906094 (adobe pdf) | ISBN
   9781119906087 (epub)
Subjects: LCSH: Goal (Psychology)
Classification: LCC BF505.G6 M36 2023 (print) | LCC BF505.G6 (ebook) |
   DDC 158.1–dc23/eng/20220708
LC record available at https://lccn.loc.gov/2022026335
LC ebook record available at https://lccn.loc.gov/2022026336

COVER DESIGN: PAUL MCCARTHY

SKY10035968_091322

To Lola.

I wish you confidence in your profound worthiness.

Contents

"We have been trained too long to strive and not to enjoy."
—*John Maynard Keynes*

"Adjustment, I think. Now that really is the story of my life."
—*Katherine May*

Introduction

OUR CULTURE IS obsessed with goals—achievement, growth, change, improvement. For a long time, I shared that obsession. But about five years ago, I started to question whether the goals I set and the constant impulse to strive for more genuinely served me. Was I happier? Was I more fulfilled? Was I a better business owner, wife, mother, daughter, friend because of the goals I held? Those were pretty easy questions to answer: no, no, and no. Then, I started to ask more difficult questions. Why do I fixate on goals? What drives my constant need for achievement? How do the goals I pursue alienate me from others and even myself?

As I explored those questions, both through personal reflection and thorough research, I came to a startling hypothesis: Maybe goal-setting doesn't work. Maybe goal-setting is wrapped up in the same stories and systems that make it such a challenge to find satisfaction and fulfillment in modern life. Maybe I need a whole new approach.

This isn't another book about how to set goals and achieve them. My guess is that you've already read quite a few. You've bought the planners, used the apps, and found yourself an accountability buddy. If you're like any of the thousands of people I've heard from over the last decade, you're probably still wondering, "Okay, but what *works*? What really works to change habits? What really works to achieve goals?

1

What really works to create plans that I can stick to or fit in all the responsibilities I have?"

I like that you ask questions! Here's the thing, though. I firmly believe that there are a lot more questions to ask before we find answers to those questions, if we even need to answer them at all. This book is about *those* questions—the questions about cultural narratives and moral systems, the questions about what hole we're trying to fill when we keep adding more responsibilities to our plates, the questions about whether society's shoulds and supposed-tos are worth pursuing, the questions about how to approach life and work in a society where so many face incredible burdens. This book is also what I've found works for me—and hundreds of others I've shared it with. It's a springboard that you can use to find what works for you, too. But before we can get there, I need to tell you a story. It's a story about me, the way my mind works, and how the analysis I share in this book isn't a product of a special talent for accomplishment, but instead a product of pain and doubt.

Shoot for the Moon

In my junior year of college, a library staff member recruited me as an independent consultant for a makeup and skincare company. I loved makeup, and I liked the idea of being in control of my income. Plus, I'd worked retail for years so I figured I had some transferable skills. I paid for my starter kit, as well as some additional samples, and attended my first meeting. That first meeting was the pep rally I didn't know I needed. The cheap hotel conference room shimmered with potential and positive energy. My confidence surged; I was going to make it.

My recruiter could tell I was ready to go all in. She invited me to be her guest at a bigger regional meeting in a bigger cheap hotel ballroom. While the first meeting was led by my recruiter's recruiter, this second meeting was hosted by someone much farther up the line. And this gathering was special because there was a guest speaker. If memory serves me, the guest speaker was a power player in the company—a woman with the fancy car of a certain color, a massive down line, and plenty of material success. As a sheltered 20-year-old, I'd never heard motivational speaking outside of alter calls at Christian rock festivals. I was transfixed. This woman seemed to have the answer to all of the life's biggest questions! And she believed that each of us in attendance had what it took to make it big. I am easily swept up by that kind of energy and rhetoric—I suppose most people are, that's why it works. And by "works," I mean that it works to stir people up and make them more susceptible to risk-taking.

After the event, as we walked toward her car, I told my recruiter how excited I was by what I'd heard. I didn't want to just sell makeup; I wanted to have it all. She reached into the trunk of her car and pulled out a cassette tape. "I think you'll like this," she said. It was a recording of a similar speaker, saying similar things—but now the motivation was on-demand. I'd play the tape over and over again. I learned that I'm the only one responsible for my success or failure. I learned that, if I worked hard enough, I could get whatever I wanted. I learned the makeup company's founder had herself said, "Shoot for the moon and you'll land among the stars." I liked that, even if it was astronomically inaccurate. It wasn't until at least a decade later that I learned the founder did not originate that phrase—she merely borrowed it from Norman Vincent Peale.

Like every multilevel marketing company, the company I signed up with has a clear way to ladder up in the organization. I liked that, too. Promotions weren't up to chance—if I wanted to move up, the requirements were right there in black and white. Each rung in the beauty ladder also came with an external reward. The first was the honor of donning a red blazer at official events. When you wore the red blazer to an event, everyone knew what rank you were—how committed you were to success. I earned my red blazer quickly and set my sights on earning a sporty little car, just like my recruiter had recently earned. My success was short-lived, though. As a college student, I just didn't know enough people to sell to or, more importantly, recruit. And as a painfully awkward and socially anxious person, I wasn't equipped to network my way to knowing more people. I was queasy about the few women I had recruited. Even though I knew it was "up to them" to succeed, I felt responsible for them. I didn't want them to have wasted their time or money because I had listened to some motivational tapes.

But sooner than later, I faced reality. I wasn't cut out for this particular grift. My recruiter convinced me not to sell my product back to the company (she was already dangerously close to losing her new car and, if I'd officially quit, she'd be on the hook for a car payment). Boxes of lotions, lipsticks, foundations, and samples sat in the closet of my mom's house for years after that. I didn't throw them away until after I graduated, got married, had a baby, and separated, moving back in with my mom. For years, those boxes were visual reminders that I wasn't good enough to succeed. Unknowingly, I carried that shame and doubt with me for years.

I'm not the first person to lose at the game of multilevel marketing (99 percent of people do). It's easy to get sold on the energy, the community, the potential—enough so that you forget the impossible math of the MLM system standing in your way. When you inevitably quit, all of the programming that you gorged yourself on in the beginning turns on you. Now, you're lazy; you're not committed; you've lost faith. In many ways, a multilevel marketing scheme is a microcosm of what many of us experience every day in our culture at large. We learn the path and visualize our success. We devour the positive messages and seek the wisdom of mentors farther up the ladder. We work hard—and harder still. And when stress or burnout or the reality of an economy that only works for a few becomes too much to bear? We step back, knowing we weren't good enough or strong enough. We didn't want it bad enough. We didn't think the right thoughts or manifest the right results. We blame ourselves because that's what we've been taught to do.

The Secret, by Rhonda Byrne, debuted in 2006 and, since, has sold over 35 million copies.[1] After Byrne appeared on *Oprah*—twice—the book and DVD flew off shelves. In fact, I remember just how fast it flew because I was managing a Borders Books and Music at the time. Case after case of the book appeared on our loading dock and, just as soon as we'd get the books out on the floor, they'd be gone again. I can also remember, early in the craze, hiding out in the backroom with a few co-workers to figure out what was going on with this book. What was all this fuss about? We suspected *The Secret* was no literary or philosophical masterpiece. I cracked open a copy and read out loud. We howled. Our suspicions were correct; *The Secret* was a great product but not a great idea. *The Secret* brought the Law of Attraction to the mass market. The Law of Attraction, according to Byrne and her ersatz academy of teachers, taught that you could have anything you wanted by thinking about and visualizing it intensely enough.[2] And any hardship or negative experience was also the result of your own manifestation. Your pessimistic thoughts and fears created your undesirable reality.

The Secret was not—*is not*, as Byrne has continued to release books, films, and three apps—an isolated craze. It's merely the slick repackaging of a message that's been bubbling in the waters of American culture for 150 years called New Thought. Early proponents of New Thought believed in the power of the mind to heal the body. As historian Kate Bowler explains, "New Thought taught that the world should be reimagined as thought rather than substance. The spiritual world formed absolute reality, while the material world was the mind's projection."[3] While New Thought's adherents, like the teachers of *The Secret*, would point to "ancient wisdom" (both Judeo-Christian beliefs and Eastern religion) as the source of their knowledge, it should be understood as a distinct, colonial, and capitalist phenomenon. New Thought didn't stop at championing the "mind-cure" for disease or the divinity of the self as true self-actualization. By the early 20th century, New Thought became a more explicitly economic teaching, too. Bowler calls this new iteration an American gospel, "based on hard work, pragmatism, innovation, self-reliance and openness to risk."

The Problem with Positive Thinking

One of the runaway bestsellers that preached this new gospel was Norman Vincent Peale's *The Power of Positive Thinking*. Peale's book is full of scriptural one-liners turned into positive affirmations, as well as "rags" to riches stories of men who were down on their luck and turned everything around once they discovered they could just think happy (and wealthy) thoughts. In the same vibrational wavelength of his pseudo-spiritual progeny, Peale writes, "The secret is to fill your mind with thoughts of faith, confidence, and security." And while I was surprised to discover that Peale is slightly more generous to structural burdens than those that came later, his book also contains nuggets like this one: "It is appalling to realize the number of pathetic people who are hampered and made miserable by the malady popularly called the inferiority complex." Or, "Disability, tension, and kindred troubles may result from a lack of inner harmony."[4] If this all sounds familiar, it's because it's woven into the fabric of our economic, cultural, and political systems today. While Peale, Byrne, and other proponents of New Thought like to remind us that our negative thoughts create undesirable realities, they are actively creating a theory of self that puts the blame for suffering and adversity on us.

If I'm to be completely responsible for my own success or lack thereof, how I respond to failure will naturally be to condemn myself. And it was from that self-loathing that one early morning at the gym, I found myself googling, "Can I change my personality?" There was a not insignificant part of me that believed I could think my way to a personality more suited to success. That it was my own deficiency of character that had led to my mental anguish. With more than five years distance from that morning, I can see how extreme and unreasonable that pervasive thought was. But I've learned since that it is simply the air we breathe in 21st-century America. It was certainly the air I was breathing at the gym—where the gospel of thinness hangs like a sweaty stench in that same air.

Now, to be clear, I am a huge supporter of mindset work. I believe that the way I think about things does impact my actions, which has the power to create the results I desire. But I don't engage with the "power of positive thinking" type of mindset work that floods our Instagram and Twitter feeds, nor do I ignore the material obstacles in my path. Instead, I hone my mindset through critical thinking and analysis. I ask copious questions and pick apart assumptions. If someone comes up with a brilliant strategy or a compelling business move, I consider what questions they asked to come up with it. I work through what base knowledge they possess that's different from my own. I don't believe that "believing in myself" is a pre-condition for rational or strategic thought. When I'm truly engaging those critical thinking skills, I'm much less likely to blame myself for failure. I'm less likely to fixate on my own shortcomings and how to overcome them. Critical thinking created a more satisfying life for me than positive thinking ever could.

There are things I wish were different about me, things that make it difficult to access what others find so worthwhile. I wish I understood others' emotions better. I wish it were easier to connect with new people. I wish I didn't find myself overstimulated and overwhelmed at conferences or parties. I wish I had a softer focus and didn't have such a hard time being interrupted or switching tasks. I wish I had just a few of the traits I so admire in others but are utterly baffled by when it comes to myself. Yet, I've also come to realize that I am satisfied without these things. I don't actually possess a deep longing for a wide circle of friends or focus better suited to multitasking. I don't need to overcome these "obstacles" because they're not truly obstacles to my satisfaction.

That said, I can't remember a time when I didn't feel a fundamental brokenness about who I am. I can't remember a time or a place when I felt like I belonged to any group or community. I often don't feel at home in my closest relationships. I am always on edge, trying to figure out what others want from me and hopelessly trying to contort myself into that shape. This unease has plagued me throughout my life. As a kid, I perpetually felt on the outside looking in. As a teen, I felt so angry at the world for not having a place for me. As a young adult, I started to feel the weight of isolation and contemplated suicide. And now, as I approach middle age, I have days when I just feel hopeless. It's probably no wonder then that I have dealt with depression and anxiety for as long as I felt separate, other, unwanted. I reached an acute awareness of whom I believe I should be to belong as well as the not-so-sneaking suspicion that I am fundamentally not that person.

Before you assume that I am a drearily unhappy person who has found no success in life, I can assure you that that's not the case. I have been known to cackle with laughter—especially at puns or cutting jokes about the difficulties of being a woman. I run two successful businesses. I am happily married to a wonderful partner, and I'm the proud mama of an absolutely incredible 14-year-old girl. In so many ways, my life is good, and I'm quite happy. I'm quite happy except when I'm not. And when I'm not is when I'm reminded just how out-of-place I am. When I'm not is when I feel like things would be so much easier if I were just a different person. This tension—between satisfaction and contentment on one side and despair on the other— confounds many people around me. I'm profoundly misunderstood because I exist somewhere on this spectrum of extremes. So again, I consider what it would take to become someone else.

Recently, I learned something about myself that brought all of this into focus: I'm autistic. Thanks to the brave first-hand accounts of women diagnosed as adults, I finally discovered the framework that makes sense of my whole experience of brokenness and not belonging.

(I'm especially grateful to Katherine May and her memoir, *The Electricity of Every Living Thing* as well as Amy Richards of the *Square Peg Podcast*.) And while this framework does nothing to fix those feelings on its own, it does give me a much healthier way of processing my difference as well as a sustainable way to understand better who I am and how I want to grow. I don't want to change who I am (though I'd be glad to know her better), but I do want to grow as a human—and a leader, a wife, a mom, and a friend. I want to practice different ways to engage with the world and make sense of what happens around me. I want to become more "me" and, maybe for the first time, discover what that truly means.

So even though my googling about personality change came up short, I can tie that cringy inspiration to the path that would lead me to discover my own process for self-exploration, growth, and satisfaction. This book is that path and my process. You don't need to be autistic to use it, and it might very well not be a perfect fit for many autistic people or other neurodivergent people. It also might not be a perfect fit for plenty of neurotypical people, people from underestimated groups, people of varied genders, or abilities, or family structures. No, I can't guarantee this process will be a perfect fit. But I can guarantee that this process is rooted in questioning everything we've ever learned about life design, goals, or planning because I've had to question everything to create my own path. Asking questions is my superpower, if I do say so myself. And I will offer you plenty of questions to ask yourself as the book unfolds. I aim to help you find the practice and process that works for the kind of growth you're looking for. I want to help give structure and meaning to growth based on curiosity instead of achievement. And, I want to show you how so much of what we've all learned about goals, productivity, and personal growth is rooted in harmful narratives about what it takes to be worthy in our modern society.

Achievement Is My Middle Name

Ultimately, my investigation of whether I could become someone different led to discovering that I had a toxic relationship to goals.

Goals had become a way for me to feel like I fit in or had something to contribute to the group. Whether I aimed to make more money, earn a new accolade, or break into a new social group, my goal provided me with a clear-cut way of engaging with the world. It helped me control the uncontrollable—which, in turn, put me at some ease in situations that would otherwise be overwhelming to me.

My history with goal-setting is complicated. On the one hand, I'm a goal-oriented overachiever obsessed with passing the next milestone on the path to success (and belonging). On the other hand, I'm prone to anxiety, burnout, and a single-mindedness that can seriously damage my relationships—all exacerbated by my attempts to reach my goals at any cost. How could I be anything else? Goal-setting is often the keystone organizing factor of our lives and work, so much so that many of us use our orientation to goals as a way to identify ourselves. We set goals, make plans, and learn how to execute—a never-ending cycle of future-focused striving. We read books on how to choose goals and make plans. We listen to the podcasts with productivity experts and mindset coaches. We watch glitzy TED talks to fuel the fire of our ambition (or the ambition we think we're supposed to have). My tendency is toward the dogged—and often neurotic—pursuit of goals, but those with a more even temperament get caught up in the frenzy, too.

Who am I without a goal? In addition to giving me a way to fit into the world, working toward a goal gave me a way to shake off the persistent sense of precarity that comes from moving through a society that seems to be on ever-shakier ground. It gives me a way to feel like I have some control over the future, some agency in how my life turns out. When I strive toward a goal, I have purpose and direction. It's how I learned to cope. And how I learned to win praise from others.

My first taste of the kind of recognition I could get from being better, smarter, or stronger came toward the end of fifth grade. I was bored out of my mind in school and I was starting to disengage. My teachers and my mom could tell there was something wrong and that, just maybe, they could do something about it. They made the decision: I would skip sixth grade and go straight to junior high school. While I've come to know that this wasn't all that out of the ordinary, it didn't happen in my school district. I was the first student the administration had allowed to skip a grade in a very long time. When I got on the bus going to the junior high school on the first day of school, the other kids tried to tell me I was on the wrong bus. I happily told them I was where I was supposed to be. At school, the gifted teacher recommended that I not tell people about skipping a grade. But enough people knew me—and knew that I didn't use to be in the same grade as them—that staying quiet was impossible. I quickly earned a reputation as the kid who skipped a grade. It wasn't a good reputation. Other kids viewed my accomplishment with a mixture of disdain, jealousy, and mild fascination. I was different, separate from the "normal" kids, and part of me liked it that way. Of course, part of me hated it, too.

I soon started to recognize that setting and achieving goals was a way to maintain my difference and separation. I liked standing apart, even if I also felt a deep desire to belong. Accomplishment gave me a way of (sort of) having both. The more I accomplished, the more I marked myself as a valuable community member and someone special. I externalized my yet unspoken feelings of brokenness and separation in every goal I set and achieved. I focused on being the first chair trombonist in high school, climbing over other players to get to the top. In college, my goal was to be in charge of the weekly worship services on campus while also being the top student in the religion department—oh, and the drum major, too. In my over-before-it-began graduate school experience, I realized that I was missing the instruction manual for achieving at that level. Worrying that I wasn't good enough for or worthy of the program that accepted me, I quit. Quitting graduate school led to work in retail. There, the siren song of promotion after promotion kept me from seeing that I was climbing a ladder that made me physically ill. My chronic depression came roaring back, and I developed a serious problem with disordered eating.

Is there something in how I describe myself and my relationship to achievement that's familiar to you? Maybe you can see yourself in it; you, too, are achievement-oriented, competitive, and ambitious. Or, maybe you see someone you love in that description—or someone you can't stand. Perhaps this description is precisely how you don't want other people to talk about you.

Five years ago, I started questioning whether building my life around goals and achievement was serving me. I wondered whether the achievements I chose for goals were based on my desire—or whether I was just trying to keep up with (or leap over) my peers. Is this really what I want? Or am I just doing what I'm supposed to do? I examined whether working toward future goals was affording me the day-to-day life that I wanted. I investigated why I often sabotaged my efforts to reach my goals and got in my own way. Ultimately, this is the path that led to me googling about changing my personality.

Again, you might be entertaining some of these questions right now, too. Or, maybe these are precisely the kind of questions that you've worked to avoid as you eschew goal-setting, competition, and ambition altogether. Either way, I think we can all agree that there's got to be a better way. Sure, goals help us make plans and structure our lives—but at what cost? There has got to be a way that allows us to find focus and balance, to give us a sense of direction and find satisfaction in our present location.

What Works?

That was the quest I set out on: to find a new way to plan, work, and organize my life that didn't revolve around externalizing deeply personal questions. This book is everything I learned in that process and the framework I now use to orient myself and my actions. Getting to this point has been a complicated learning process. Being an achievement-oriented, hyper-competitive, winning-is-my-personal-identity type of person has given me a way to make sense of myself in the world. Setting goals and racing toward the finish line was just how I functioned. So disrupting those habits and dismantling the frameworks I've always relied on led to some pretty dark and disorienting moments. I had to come to terms with the fact that I'd never seen a shiny medal I didn't want to win. And, I had to reckon with the fact that chasing medals and merit badges damaged or destroyed relationships that I value. But what I found at the deepest layer of my inquiry was a quest for worthiness. The promotions, scholarships, leadership roles, and partnerships were progressively more damaging attempts to prove myself worthy. I wanted to have definitive proof that I was good enough. And I wanted evidence that maybe, just maybe, I was exceptional. I hoped that with every step up the ladder I took, I'd be a little closer to feeling like I was going to be okay.

To work my way up the ladder, I would identify the next goal I needed to check off and then—always with limited information—calculate the fastest path to that achievement without regard for long-term ramifications. That meant I often found myself perched precariously on a ladder I didn't want to be on top of. But I felt compelled to just keep climbing. The drive to prove myself worthy of another step up dominated how I approached life, work, and even play. And it made me sick.

At this point, you're probably either nodding along thinking, "Yeah, me too," or you're thinking, "Whoa, that's messed up." Maybe, you're thinking both. It's taken a lot of work to get to the point where I can look back on my own story and see both sides. Ultimately, all of the striving toward worthiness, yearning to belong, and chasing other people's goals led, predictably, to burnout. That, combined with the devastating 2016 election, forced me to contemplate where I was and how I'd gotten there. When I tell the story, I always point to this time as the turning point—my wake-up call for finding a new way to organize my life. But of course, it was quite the process to start dismantling all of the narratives, assumptions, and conditioning that I had about myself and the world. I'd venture to say that I still have a long way to go, yet the vantage point I have now has proven valuable to others.

So this book is the full story of my deconstruction, told through the lens of culture, commitment, practice, and process. It's how I discovered what kept me from going all-in on my life and pursuing what mattered to me. It's also an interactive guide for deconstructing your own relationship to goals and the quest for worthiness. It's a blueprint for personal evolution without the compulsion to set higher goals or seek new ways to prove yourself. And finally, it's a look at how changing the way we show up in the world can positively impact our communities.

My goal for this book has been to explore how we can use personal growth to foster community growth. My editor pointed out the irony of noting that I have a "goal" for this book when what I'm trying to do is critique the whole culture of goal-setting. I laughed out loud when I read her comment. In most cases, I find other words that fit when using "goal" might be appropriate (e.g., aim, target, objective). I'm not anti-goal. I'm anti-Goal. We'll always have goals of one sort or another—and while I might use different language, I do acknowledge that, at some point, it becomes a matter of semantics. What I do take a position against an individualist, ableist, pseudo-religious construction of Goals. I stand for critical thinking about our goals— where they come from, who or what they really serve, and how we might be taking on cultural shoulds and supposed-tos that harm us and our communities.

Most books that deal with goals, personal improvement, or productivity treat the individual as the source of both challenges and solutions. I want to offer an alternative, an approach that recognizes the structural issues and cultural context that make life harder than it needs to be. My hope is that you come to this book not looking for positive affirmations or a no-fail guide to success, but with an open mind, ready to explore some territory you might not have explored before. I believe that personal growth doesn't have to lead only to individual success. Personal growth can help us activate our communities, families, and friendships—the positive effects of which come back to us in spades. adrienne maree brown put it this way: "How we live and grow and stay purposeful in the face of constant change actually does determine both the quality of our lives, and the impact that we can have when we move into action together."[5]

In the first two chapters, I explore how we've gotten to this point and why the experiences I describe are so universally familiar—whether through lived experience or observation. We venture down The Validation Spiral as well as detangle the threads of rugged individualism, Protestant work ethic, and supremacy culture that shape our goal-setting impulses.

In Chapter 3, I unpack how our identities become wrapped up in the goals we set and the way those goals are performed for others, with special attention on how the internet has encouraged that performance. In Chapter 4, I contrast how we do things differently when we're focused on future achievement versus when we're present to daily practice and process. I'll also give you a better look at what it means to be "all in" when it comes to your life and work. Chapter 5 is all about understanding our capacity—the resources we have and how we use them.

Chapters 6 through 10 contain the process I've created to organize my life around practice and process instead of goals. You'll learn how setting commitments about how you want to show up can change your life, as they've changed mine, and you'll explore how to give your life and work strategic direction without fixating on specific goals. You'll create your own comprehensive framework to guide your growth and organize your work.

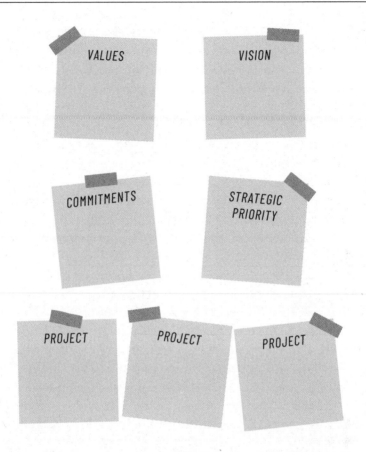

The final chapter offers guidance on follow-through, self-sabotage, and behavior change. I also talk about what happens when you inevitably can't stick to your plan and why that's a very good thing. And last, I offer you a few more tools for thinking critically about your choices and discovering what works for you.

If you've started to question whether bigger goals, longer work hours, or productivity hacks are the best way to organize your life, you're in the right place. If you've started to wonder whether it's really your responsibility to "fix" the ways you are "broken," this is for you. You might not yet have any idea what you want instead, and that's perfectly understandable. When I started to ask these same questions, I didn't have much of a grasp on specifics, either. I just had a persistent inkling that I'd gotten way off course and needed to recalibrate. I yearned for a better way to be all in for myself *and* my community. And I'm betting that you feel—to one degree or another—similarly.

Since then, my life has been full of reflection, analysis, and awareness-building. While I'm more sure than ever that I don't want to climb the ladder anymore, I know that my default mode is still to try to ascend. My identity is still tightly wrapped around each rung. Every day is an opportunity to practice satisfaction rather than striving. Recently, I heard Sonya Renee Taylor, author of *The Body Is Not an Apology*, talk about our drive to climb the ladder. A line she said has stuck with me—boring itself into my very being. Taylor said, "The ladder is real only because we keep trying to climb it."[6]

The aim of this book isn't just to help you ignore the ladder or whatever yardstick you use to measure your worthiness. It's to show you how these measures don't even exist in the first place, and demonstrate that your worthiness doesn't come from how high you rise or how far you go but because you exist. There is no higher or lower. There is no better or worse. There is no stronger or weaker. As we continue to reset our expectations and assumptions, we can take stock of what's truly important to us—to our businesses, to our work, to our families, and our communities—instead of constantly taking stock of how we measure up or how much higher we have to climb. When we see that there is no ladder, we can finally go all-in on the life and work that matters most to us.

1

The Validation Spiral

I couldn't shake the feeling of precariousness—that all that I'd worked for could just disappear—or reconcile it with an idea that had surrounded me since I was a child: that if I just worked hard enough, everything would pan out.
—Anne Helen Petersen, *Can't Even: How Millennials Became the Burnout Generation*[7]

"BINGO!" I HEARD my classmate call out. I started to feel my eyes well up with tears.

My second-grade teacher noticed. She guided me out of the classroom and into the hall. She gently asked why on earth I was crying over a game of bingo. As only a precocious 8-year-old could, I tried to explain that I hated bingo because it required no skill. It was pure luck. There was no strategy to employ, no natural talent to rely on to win. Either your numbers were called or they weren't. I couldn't extract value out of a win. There was no meaning to victory—although loss still hurt. My teacher gently explained that it was "just a game" and encouraged me to enjoy it. But that's the thing. There has been nothing in my life that has been "just a game." Every win was a small indication that things would work out, that I'd be okay. Every loss was a devastating reminder that I could lose everything—and probably would.

17

What I couldn't quite explain at the time was that there was no way I could parlay a game of bingo into validation that I was good enough. Today, I know this feeling—this fear—well. It's with me all the time. I'm self-conscious to admit that this continues to be an issue for me. I'm much more aware of it now, and I course correct much more quickly. But in owning the fact that I still struggle, my hope is that this story (and this whole book, really) doesn't get thrown into the mountainous pile of stories of overcoming. I don't believe that we're supposed to transcend all of our challenges—congenital or cultural. I believe that recognizing the persistence of these challenges is key to maintaining our awareness as well as acting to collectively to make change. I constantly seek ways to prove myself good enough and validate my worthiness. I used to worry that I fixated on demonstrating that I was better than others, but I've come to realize that, instead, I'm just trying to prove that I belong. And that it's okay for me to take up space.

I seek validation of my worth, my usefulness, my value in everything. And I'm not alone. Validation-seeking is one of the defining pathologies of our culture. How could it not be? We move through social circles with the brand names we buy. We attempt to one-up each other by what we post on social media. We strive for more and better at work, at home, and at play. We're desperately seeking a way to figure out whether our numbers will get called or whether someone else is going to yell "BINGO!" long before we can cover up the squares.

The Question of Worthiness

Why is validation so elusive? Why do we organize our lives and work to prove to others (and ourselves) that we're worthy of love, respect, and belonging? Because we've been taught to question our worthiness. And while this isn't a new phenomenon, it gained a new flavor over the last century or so.

In 1947, a group of leaders in the fields of economics, sociology, and history gathered at a ski resort on Mont Pelerin in Switzerland. They were there to discuss what they saw as harmful overreach by the governments of Western Europe and the United States. That harmful overreach? It was government programs like Social Security and unemployment insurance as well as regulations on business and industry. Western democracies increasingly leaned toward democratic socialism, and this group was quite concerned. The Mont Pelerin Society, as the group would come to be known, advocates a hands-off approach to economic policy. The group believes that private enterprise and free markets can provide better solutions than governments. Its approach is in direct opposition to Keynesian economics and Marxist philosophy, and its aims would be familiar to anyone who consumes the smallest amount of political news in the United States.[8]

Friedrich Hayek was one of the organizers of this original conference. Hayek was an advocate for individualism and self-reliance over socialism or collectivism. He believed that free society—and free markets—would create better outcomes than one that was planned or designed for desired outcomes: "If left free, men will often achieve more than individual human reason could design or foresee." Who is going to argue with liberty, am I right? As he started to draw conclusions about how to apply this philosophy, though, things got a little weird. In *Individualism and Economic Order*, Hayek writes:

> . . .only because men are in fact unequal can we treat them equally. If all men were completely equal in their gifts and inclinations, we should have to treat them differently in order to achieve any sort of social organization. Fortunately, they are not equal; and it is only owing to this that the differentiation of functions need not be determined by the arbitrary decision of some organizing will but that, after creating formal equality of the rules applying in the same manner to all, we can leave each individual to find his own level. There is all the difference in the world between treating people equally and attempting to make them equal.[9]

What Hayek suggests here is that if everyone were equal, we'd need the state to determine our responsibilities—choose our occupations, determine our wages, maybe even select our homes or families. While dystopian novelists have long envisioned destructive systems in this vein and dictators like Stalin, Mao, and the Kim family put them into practice, it's hardly true of the direction Western democracies took in the early 20th century. Instead, those nations took steps to treat more people equally—white women finally got the right to vote, chattel slavery ended, and workers started to gain some protections and the right to collective bargaining.

Hayek, of course, worked at a time when the illusory veil of a monocultural nation had yet to be lifted. He was "free" to allow his arguments to pertain to the white, educated, property-owning upper class man. He was unburdened by the structural inequities faced by women, workers, former enslaved people, or immigrants. He could easily explain away their poverty, lack of rights, or lack of opportunities as a function of their "gifts and inclinations," rather than a product of a system that favored people like him: ". . .the relative remunerations the individual can expect from the different uses of his abilities and resources correspond to the relative utility of the result of his efforts to others but also that these remunerations correspond to the objective results of his efforts rather than to their subjective merits." Your economic conditions, then, are the product of your interests, talents, and *value to society*.

This, then, might be the genesis of our contemporary concern with worthiness and validation. Hayek and his buddies in the Mont Pelerin Society, including economist Milton Friedman, the figurehead of conservative economics in the United States, have had a profound and long-lasting effect on our cultural narrative. The authors of *Confidence Culture*, Shani Orgad and Rosalind Gill, described the cultural impact of this movement, known today as neoliberalism, as a "hegemonic, quotidian sensibility." They argued that the machine Hayek set in motion transformed us into entrepreneurs-by-necessity, "hailed by rules that emphasize ambition, calculation, competition, self-optimization, and personal responsibility."[10]

Anything less than the successful organization of your life around those factors is a personal failing, a deficit in your usefulness to society. You see the evidence of this in the hoops someone has to go through to apply for disability or even unemployment assistance. You see it in the "means testing" that gets baked into every piece of legislation designed to help people move out of poverty. It's baked into performance reviews, the gig-ification of the workforce, and stagnant wages. You even see it in the way different fields of study are treated at the college level. The department I graduated from was eliminated a couple of years ago in order to siphon its funding into a multimillion-dollar sports medicine and physical therapy building. The message? Sports medicine practitioners and physical therapists are worth more to society than philosophers and theologians. What's more, if you venture onto any social media platform, you can witness the *performance* of usefulness and worthiness to rake in those validating likes.

Maybe today, faced with a distinctly multicultural society and hard evidence of how free markets do *not* create level playing fields for people, Hayek might draw different conclusions. Maybe he would accept that privatization has exacerbated inequality and lack of freedom for many. But his work, along with others', in the first half of the 20th century fomented a whole movement which, in practice, has created a pathological fear of unworthiness aimed to keep us striving, consuming, and climbing over others on the way up the ladder. It's from within this movement that other questions of worthiness arise, most often around gender, disability, and race.

As a woman, I learned a host of shoulds and supposed-tos that would prove my worthiness. I should attain a body that conforms to white, straight Western beauty standards. I'm supposed to see my value in finding a husband and caring for a family. The after-effects of second-wave feminism conditioned me to measure myself against standards that are traditionally coded male so that I could prove I was worthy of being a 21st-century woman. Men deal with the question of worthiness, too. They're socialized to pursue becoming the "alpha" of their friend groups. They're taught to see their value in their ability to provide for a family financially or claim the sexiest mate. They're conditioned to measure their worthiness against their title at work or the car they drive. And, of course, that only begins to account for the social conditioning of nondisabled, cis-gendered, heterosexual, neurotypical people. When you add disability, nonconforming gender, queerness, immigrant status, or neurodivergence into the mix, the weight of the pressure to "measure up" can be too much to bear. Race adds a whole other element to account for.

Lucky for us, thanks to the legacy of individualism (which I'll explore more in Chapter 2), even the way we process our anxiety about worthiness has a pathology. We call it the "Imposter Syndrome," the feeling that you are not good enough and soon to be found out as a fraud. This phenomenon was first described by Pauline Rose Clance and Suzanne Imes in 1978.[11] Imposter Syndrome has most often been characterized as an individual condition—a mysterious questioning of ability despite all indicators to the contrary which disproportionately impacts high-achieving women. However, seeing Impostor Syndrome as an individual condition belies the very real, very loud messages that women and underestimated groups receive, telling them that, if we were really good enough, we'd already be doing better than we are.

It often feels like the only way to answer the question of worthiness is through external validation—and achieving bigger and better goals is one of our primary ways of doing that. In smaller ways, we also seek validation in our daily commitments and responsibilities. By saying "yes" to more and more, we can feel more useful and more worthy of the part we play in our families, our workplaces, and our communities. That is until it all starts to get too much, and we hurtle toward burnout. One of the ways we can see this cultural pattern most clearly is by how we overcommit and overschedule ourselves.

"I'm busy!"

We live in a chronically overcommitted culture. We say "yes" to too many things. We pack our calendars full of life and business commitments. We pin our hopes on doing it all. We're fried and frazzled from just trying to keep up with our commitments. We're stretched beyond our capacity. You'd think that the exhaustion and anxiety caused by this state of affairs would be enough for us to put an end to it. But very few of us reach that conclusion on our own because "saying yes" is one of the primary ways we seek the external validation that temporarily pacifies our inner struggle. Without all of the excess commitment and responsibility, we lose a crucial way to reassure ourselves that we're doing okay, that we're still productive members of society.

Our culture celebrates the entrepreneur who sleeps four hours per night and the single mom who works two jobs to keep food on the table. We're afraid to be seen as lazy, unproductive, or coasting. The more we say "yes" to, the more we can expect to be lauded for our efforts and validated in our contributions. Saying "yes" gives us another chance at hearing our number called in the bingo game of life. But, as

I'm sure you've realized by now, this causes some problems—a phenomenon I call "The Validation Spiral."

Deja Vu All Over Again

The Validation Spiral starts in that all-too-familiar place: saying "yes" over and over again. It might sound like, "Yes, I'll bring the cookies to softball practice even though I'll be coming straight from work," or "Yes, I'll head up another project outside of my job description," or "Yes, I'll take on another client even though I'm already working 60 hours per week." We seek validation for our worthiness and usefulness in our families, in our jobs, in our friendships, and even in the quiet moments we call "me time." At first, the extra responsibilities and commitments seem harmless. The inconvenience or time feels like an appropriate trade-off for feeling helpful, like a valuable member of the team. Every time someone asks you to step up or help out, you feel like you belong.

But over time, those commitments start to add up. We fill our capacity to overflowing and stretch our resources thin. We might feel resentful of the people who have asked us for help or angry at ourselves for always saying "yes." Despite the growing exhaustion and bad feelings, we push on. We struggle against labels like unhelpful, difficult, or lazy—labels we are all too quick to put on ourselves. We push on until we can't anymore. Maybe we get sick, or we relapse into a mental illness or addiction. Perhaps insomnia brings us to our knees. Maybe we end up burned out and unable to cope with all of the responsibilities.

Burnout, by the way, is a studied phenomenon, not simply a term for being stressed out and exhausted. Burnout is the result of overwhelming stress on the body—including the nervous system. The stress doesn't have to be overwhelming in terms of acute magnitude—a divorce, diagnosis, or job loss. The overwhelming stress that causes burnout is often an overwhelming *accumulation* of stress. In other words, all those yeses add up to psychological and physiological consequences. Herbert Freudenberger studied burnout among "caring professions" in the mid-1970s. He characterized the condition as emotional exhaustion, decreased sense of accomplishment, and depersonalization. Essentially,

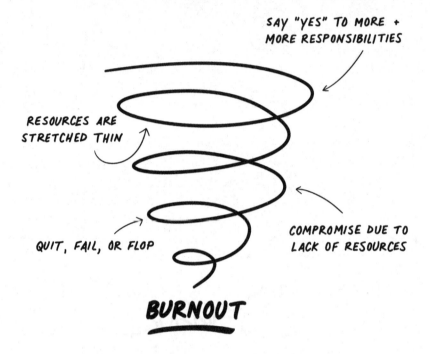

THE VALIDATION SPIRAL

SAY "YES" TO MORE +
MORE RESPONSIBILITIES

RESOURCES ARE
STRETCHED THIN

QUIT, FAIL, OR FLOP

COMPROMISE DUE TO
LACK OF RESOURCES

BURNOUT

when we burn out, we've cared too much for too long, seen a lack of impact from our actions, and burned the empathy candle at both ends.[12]

Burnout is the more intense of two inevitable results of endless validation-seeking (the other being undercommitment, which I'll explain in the next section). We give and strive to prove our worthiness to others—and ourselves. We give and persevere until we're exhausted, ineffective, and resentful. In their book *Burnout: The Secret to Unlocking the Stress Cycle*, Drs. Emily and Amelia Nagoski describe how our bodies fight back against all of the stress we impose on ourselves while our fear of selfishness or laziness compels us to continue capitulating to new responsibilities. They write that our "instinct for self-preservation is battling a syndrome that insists that self-preservation is selfish, so your efforts to care for yourself might actually make things worse, activating even more punishment from the world or from yourself because how dare you?"

In our culture, women and marginalized people experience the imperative to overgive, overdeliver, and overcommit to the most significant degree. But no one is immune to the ways that uncertainty, complexity, and emotional labor can contribute to burning out. Journalist Anne Helen Petersen documents the universality of burnout among millennials in her book *Can't Even: How Millennials Became the Burnout Generation*. Petersen's analysis feels spot-on to me—we're the same age—but it also resonates with many who were born before 1980. Burnout isn't some quirk of psychology in the 21st century. It's the product of a system that hasn't worked and won't work for anyone but the wealthiest and most powerful. Wage stagnation, unhealthy work expectations, precarious employment structures—not to mention the erosion of any assistance from the government if things go south— makes it difficult to feel a modicum of comfort, let alone attain success. Petersen writes, "The only way to make it all work is to employ relentless focus—to never, ever stop moving."

Undercommitment

Most of us, I think, are familiar with the potential for burnout and its costs. We can recognize it in others and maybe even in ourselves. But burnout is just the more evident result of our quest to prove ourselves worthy and useful. The other way overcommitment and validation-seeking plays out is seemingly more banal, less deserving of intervention: undercommitment. While burnout may put us on the sidelines, undercommitment keeps us in the game but doesn't allow us to play our best. Undercommitment is what happens when we lack the necessary resources to carry out the responsibilities we've said "yes" to. When we've overcommitted ourselves on the whole, we're bound to be undercommitted to any individual endeavor. Opting to overcommit means opting out of the ability to be all-in on what you're committed to. We might think we're following through and holding up our commitments, but we also end up with disappointing results because we just couldn't invest the time or effort required for better results. I mean, what else could we expect? We had to parcel out our reserves of time and effort between the multitude of things we said "yes" to despite being overscheduled and exhausted already.

In my work with small business owners, I see the phenomenon of undercommitment all the time. The folks I work with are passionate, effective people. They care deeply about their work and the people they serve. But they worry that they're not doing enough, that what they've created isn't good enough, and that the businesses they've built aren't strong enough. So they push themselves to do more and more. They end up with highly complicated plans and overcrowded calendars. So they divide up their limited resources among all the things they think they're supposed to be doing to maintain the perception that they're doing this whole business thing right. The result? Everything they do is a half-measure: the social media posts, the sales calls, the product development. They don't get great results because they can't pursue anything they do with the proper resources. If you don't have the capacity or resources to devote to what you've committed to, whatever you're doing won't work, even if your plan is sound (more on capacity and resources in Chapter 5). Undercommitment can be difficult to identify while you're in it, though. And it can be tough to spot when the stakes are as high as they are when we're working through our responsibilities to business, career, or family. Instead, we internalize the results of undercommitment (e.g., lackluster results, missed opportunities, resentment) and use them as evidence of our own personal failings.

I first started to notice my undercommitment pattern outside of work or family. I noticed it in sports. I played a bunch of sports as a kid and early teen. In high school, I started to focus more on school and music to prepare for college, so sports took a (very) backseat. Two decades passed before I reacquainted myself with my inner athlete. It was love at second sight. I started running. Then I learned bouldering— which is climbing on short walls or big rocks with no ropes. From there, I started powerlifting and practicing yoga. Working out helped me deal with my anxiety, and training for new performance milestones gave me a sense of, you guessed it, validation.

I put a lot of time into fitness and sports. But even so, it was a challenge to effectively divide my resources among running, lifting, climbing, and yoga. At first, I tried to improve my performance in each discipline concurrently. Early on, this was possible—not because I was training effectively but simply because I was training instead of sitting on the couch. As time went on and my general performance improved, I found it more and more difficult to improve my performance in any individual pursuit. I tried to run faster, lift heavier, climb harder, and flow more gracefully all at the same time—failing miserably. I was always sore, constantly tired, and always on the verge of injury. Even though sports were a low-stakes venture for me, I still felt like I failed— which meant I pushed myself even harder.

I realized that I was undercommitted to what I was trying to accomplish because I overcommitted to performance goals. The remedy was to prioritize my training better so that I was only focused on one performance goal at a time—and then use the other disciplines for cross-training or pleasure. For instance, if I set a goal to run a half marathon, I'd scale back my weightlifting and climbing goals so that

I could focus on my running endurance. If I had a climbing competition coming up, I'd scale back on running and lifting to focus on strength endurance and technique for climbing. I fully committed my resources—time, energy, muscle—to one thing at a time and didn't worry about leaving some in reserve for other goals. Focusing on my commitment to just one sport or performance goal at a time had the added benefit of making sure I was never bored with how I trained. I enjoyed it more, and I was more effective.

Sports became the training ground for how I approached all of my responsibilities. I started to see that I couldn't commit to the performance improvements in everything I had said "yes" to. I just didn't have the resources (no one does). Sports are low-stakes, though. I'm not a professional athlete, and I haven't tied my self-worth to whether I can crack running a 5K in less than 23 minutes or not. It was relatively easy for me to dial back my performance targets and focus on one thing at a time. It's not so easy when it comes to work or family. The things we've said "yes" to for work or family have much higher stakes. The shoulds and supposed-tos mix with our fear of not being good enough. We have a sense of identity around responsibilities to work and family, and the validation we seek from them is often central to how we understand our self-worth. So undercommitment continues to be a persistent problem. As we divvy up our resources among #allthethings and become less effective across the board, we feel less useful and less validated. So what do we do? We pursue new responsibilities and projects. We say "yes" again and again, chasing that feeling of validation and worthiness.

And we descend another layer into the spiral.

How Goals Fuel the Spiral

When I started to identify The Validation Spiral in my own life, I wondered what was wrong with me. Was I so broken inside that I had to chase after the approval of others? What undiagnosed psychological condition was causing me to prove my usefulness to society? What maladapted personality trait caused me to continually compromise on my commitments? Since learning that I'm autistic, I've realized that my neurology has likely exacerbated my experience of the cultural imperative of validation through accomplishment. According to a study by Amy Pearson and Kieran Rose in the journal *Autism in Adulthood*, autistic masking is often a contributing factor to burnout. They find that, to avoid external consequences (e.g., being looked over for a promotion), autistic people may try to "pass as normal" and defy their own innate behaviors. But "passing" (or masking) brings with it greater *internal* consequences, like burnout.[13] I've certainly found this to be true for myself. But autism is not the source of my need for validation.

At first, identifying The Validation Spiral pattern led to a flood of judgment and self-critique. It was deeply unsettling. Researching whether I could change my personality was partially inspired by wanting to rid myself of the spiral and alleviate the constant anxiety that I would never be as smart or accomplished as I desperately wanted to be. And, it seemed that I was the problem. If I could change my personality—become more carefree, more social, more fun—then, surely, I could break out of the cycle. I wouldn't have to rely on the approval or validation of others to feel like I belonged. I'd just belong. Looking back on it now, this seems like a big jump to make. But in the compromise-or-burn-out part of the cycle, fixing the problem-that-was-me was all I had to go on.

The more I investigated my patterns, the more I started to wonder if maybe—just maybe—the problem wasn't with me. Maybe the problem was with how I had learned to operate in the world. The pattern wasn't a defect of my personality; it was a product of self-preservation. The Validation Spiral is how I learned to cope in a world that was begging me to question my worthiness and prove my usefulness. And I also discovered that while being neurodivergent, as well as being a woman, was making the effects of The Validation Spiral more intense, it was something that almost everyone I met dealt with in one way or another. We were all trying to keep up with cultural expectations, stretching to the breaking point to prove ourselves. Once I realized that most people dealt with this pattern to varying degrees, I identified that it wasn't me that was the problem. It was cultural and systemic. In the next chapter, I dig into how underlying cultural forces—like rugged individualism, Protestant work ethic, and supremacy culture—create the conditions that force us to create these coping mechanisms. But for now, I want to explore how goal-setting contributes to The Validation Spiral.

Shirin Eskandani studied to be an opera singer from the time she was young to all the way through college. She moved to New York City to pursue her dream—singing in Carmen at the Metropolitan Opera. While studying opera as a young singer, Eskandani was a big fish in a small pond. But moving to New York City meant that equally talented, equally persistent singers surrounded her. Her confidence was shaken, and she started to question whether she was good enough to achieve her goals. Eskandani persisted. She told me that she believed that, once she got the call to sing in Carmen, she'd know that she was good enough. She'd feel validated in her talent and hard work. When she did finally get the call, a wave of recognition hit her—one that will be familiar to anyone who has tied a sense of worthiness to the achievement of a particular goal. She realized that she still didn't feel good enough despite her accomplishment. There was no revelation of worthiness—just an empty feeling that she would need an even bigger goal to chase.[14]

It's not just the daily responsibilities and projects to which we say "yes" that keep us trapped in The Validation Spiral. It's also the very goals we organize our lives around. As an elder Millennial, my childhood was organized around getting into a good college. A wave of my Validation Spiral started by saying "yes" to the pursuit of excellent grades and enriching extracurricular activities. AP English? Yes! AP Latin? You bet! Independent-study music theory? Sure! Wind ensemble, Latin club, jazz combo, drum major in the marching band? Yes, yes, yes, and yes. I applied to a well-regarded, small, liberal arts college and won an academic scholarship as well as a music scholarship. It still wasn't enough. Double major? That sounds promising. Chapel worship leader? That might work. Honors thesis? Of course. Just like Eskandani, I kept expecting that the next accomplishment would finally put the need to prove myself to rest. But it never did.

Finally, my top choice graduate school sent me a thick envelope with an acceptance letter and an offer to cover the full cost of tuition. This was it; I was finally on the Ph.D. track. Surely, this would be enough. Instead, a tidal wave of fear and anxiety of whether I was worthy of my position in the program crashed over me. Two weeks before I was going to move into my tiny studio apartment and start school, I withdrew. Call it compromise or call it burnout—it was one of the lowest periods of my life. I was undoubtedly experiencing complete emotional exhaustion as well as feeling distinctly unaccomplished (despite literally accomplishing a huge goal). And that, combined with the worst bout of clinical depression I had experienced to date, meant that I just didn't have the resources to keep going. I took a full-time job in retail management, and the quest for validation started all over again.

Our culture teaches us to organize our lives around goals like these: the perfect role, the dream school, the sought-after title, the wedding, the purchase of a home. The shoulds and supposed-tos become a way to grade ourselves. Meditation teacher Sebene Selassie writes in her brilliant book *You Belong*, "We learn that appreciation, acceptance, and sometimes even love are connected to how we measure up."[15] Aiming for milestones can undoubtedly be a valuable way to organize our time and action. However, when the goal is a stand-in for validation that you're good enough or a symbol of your identity, the goal can pull you out of your life instead of helping you live it. We often conflate goals with the pursuit of purpose or meaning in life. Then, when we experience the results of working toward that goal (whether we hit it or not), we are left a little lost and confused. Everything isn't different on the other side of that goal. The same questions and concerns about our worthiness remain. We feel unmoored and out of balance until we can find a new goal to organize our lives around—and plunge ourselves back into The Validation Spiral.

Before we can look at how to exit The Validation Spiral and find purpose in practice instead of outcomes and achievement, we need to take an even closer look at the cultural foundations of this problem. While it might fall on us as individuals to deal with and move past the ramifications of The Validation Spiral in our own lives, it's important to understand just how much this is not a problem with us as individuals. It's a social condition that's hoisted on us through pervasive cultural narratives. To break the cycle, we must deconstruct those stories.

Reflection:

- When you were a kid, what did you believe a "successful" life looked like? What influenced your belief?
- Consider a big goal that you set in the past. Why did you set it? How did accomplishing or not accomplishing it make you feel? What story did you tell yourself about accomplishing or not accomplishing your goal?
- In what ways are you overcommitted right now? In what ways are you undercommitted?
- Are you more likely to push yourself to burnout or compromise so you can keep going? Why?

2

Why Are We So Obsessed with Goals?

. . .the most striking continuity between the old religion and the new positive thinking lies in their common insistence on work—the constant internal work of self-monitoring.

—Barbara Ehrenreich, *Bright-Sided: How Positive Thinking is Undermining America*[16]

EVERY YEAR, MILLIONS of people create New Year's resolutions, set new goals, or dream up intentions for how they'll do things better on their next trip around the sun. And while plenty of people *don't* actively partake in this ritual, the "New Year, New You" energy is still part of the cultural air we breathe. We can't avoid the recycled headlines about how to finally stick to your resolutions this year or how to make a plan to accomplish your biggest goals. Stores fill their displays with exercise equipment, planners, productivity books, and motivational journals. We are bombarded by the societal imperative to make this year better than last—to reach higher, work harder, and achieve our dreams.

Now, I'm certainly not the first person to question the wisdom of this tsunami of goal-setting advice. But I wanted to go further than questioning. I wanted to know why it seems so difficult to envision a way to live and work outside of this paradigm of continuous improvement. As a former religious studies student, I am trained to examine the underlying beliefs that make up our worldviews. I had a hunch that our obsession with goals and achievement wasn't some fluke of genetic programming. Instead, it might hinge on cultural, political, and religious programming. So maybe more like memetic programming? We think of memes as funny pictures with often nonsensical captions in Impact font overlaid on them. But really, a meme is a small segment of culture—like a gene is a small segment of DNA. The stories we absorb from fiction, history, religion, and family are memetic markers for certain beliefs. The field of memetics applies an evolutionary model to the study of culture.

I uncovered an evolution of cultural DNA that reproduces to consolidate power in a small group of people while convincing everyone else that conforming to those patterns is a moral imperative. What's more, we can see a metanarrative of "overcoming" that links these patterns together to create an almost inescapable sense that we're not enough as we are.

I'll admit that my analysis here is biased toward the culture of the United States, and biased further to the dominant, economically privileged culture here. But, while different cultural patterns may influence this paradigm in other parts of the world or even in different communities within the United States, culture is one of the United States' biggest exports. So the prevailing patterns in the United States become part of the cultural patterns elsewhere and applying this analysis, even in part, will help to better understand our relationship to goal-setting elsewhere. I'll start with the most familiar and modern pattern and then trace its lineage back through our cultural history.

Winners and Losers

I grew up a Trekkie. One of the first movies I can remember going to see in the theater was *Star Trek VI: The Undiscovered Country*. My family anxiously awaited each new episode of *Star Trek: The Next Generation* while consuming the reruns that aired in the early evening hours. We dove headfirst into *Deep Space Nine* and *Voyager* as soon as they came out.

I loved the techno-utopian dream of people from different races and even different species all working toward the goal of discovery on equal footing. In *Star Trek: First Contact*, the Next Generation crew ends up in 2063, over 300 years before the series' main timeline. Captain Picard tries to explain how the 24th-century economy works to one of the refugees they encounter on the surface of Earth. He says, "The acquisition of wealth is no longer a driving force in our lives." Instead, he says, they're driven by the desire to make themselves better and to make humanity better. That sounded pretty good to me as a 14-year-old. Heck, it sounds pretty good to me as a 40-year-old. You could pursue whatever you want to pursue without having to worry about surviving.

First Contact premiered the same year that the Personal Responsibility and Work Opportunity Act passed under the guidance of President Bill Clinton. Clinton, a Democrat, had promised to reform the welfare system, which had seen its rolls increase by a third during the recession of the early 1990s. This act, coming on the heels of Reaganomics and a push to dismantle the legacy of the New Deal, aimed to change the very foundation of welfare benefits in the United States. It was this bill that codified the "welfare to work" philosophy—shifting the core of the American consciousness to expect that government benefits should always be limited and contingent on an effort to get off of benefits. Welfare, and other public assistance programs, politicians argued, should always be a last resort. Politicians and pundits reminded us that if we needed government help to survive, well then our discipline and work ethic were deficient.[17]

While this reform passed under Clinton, it was Reagan—along with Margaret Thatcher in the United Kingdom—who set the ball in motion. Before there could be the Personal Responsibility and Work Opportunity Act, there had to be the mythic "welfare queen." In inventing the welfare queen, Reagan made an example of Linda Taylor, a mom from Chicago who had committed welfare fraud repeatedly. As Reagan told the story, Taylor conned the government out of over $150,000 in tax-free benefits in one year. However, in 1974, a grand jury indicted her for just $8,865.67 in fraud. It cost the local government $50,000 to convict her.[18]

The story of the welfare queen became a sort of anti-fable, a story designed to shame some people into doing better and convince others of their moral superiority. Reaganomics and Thatcherism convinced us that if we weren't getting by, we hadn't worked hard enough or taken enough responsibility for ourselves. Never mind structural inequality or vastly different access to opportunities, failure to thrive was a moral failing, a personal deficiency. How many nights of sleep have been lost to the fear inspired by this message? I myself have lost plenty! "The fact that capitalism has colonized the dreaming life of the population is so taken for granted that it is no longer worthy of comment," writes Mark Fisher in his book *Capitalist Realism*.[19]

It's not like Reagan or Thatcher invented this ideology, though. They simply applied it to the world's most powerful democracies. They became figureheads for rhetoric that made it impossible to remember that the United States and the United Kingdom were once invested in extending the public good rather than freeing the marketplace (that impossibility is the "realism" in Fisher's capitalist realism). Neoliberal political and economic philosophy is the evolution of those early Mont Pelerin Society conversations we discuss in Chapter 1. Until the neoliberal movement gained power, the prevailing economic theory was that of John Maynard Keynes—the guy who gave us the prediction we'd only work 15 hours a week by the turn of the 21st century.[20] Keynesian economics favored government intervention—the kind that helped see us through the Great Depression, establish workers' rights, and even provide relief during the early months of the COVID-19 pandemic. While Keynesian economics is still with us in many ways, neoliberalism has taken the reins in terms of political rhetoric and popular understanding of our responsibilities as citizens. Friedrich Hayek and Milton Friedman, with their ideas about limiting government and turning over most functions (e.g., the post office and healthcare) to the private sector, won the day at least when it comes to how we think about the role of government in the economy. At least in the United States, it's the air we breathe. Echoing the characterization of Orgad and Gill from Chapter 1, feminist philosopher Nancy Fraser describes this neoliberal capitalism as, "no mere economic system but something larger: an institutionalized social order."[21]

As you can probably tell, I have strong political beliefs. But my goal here isn't to convince you of a particular political position. My aim is to decode the political philosophy that makes up a huge part of our personal operating systems. I'm a lifelong liberal who is only getting more progressive as I get older. But I still find myself running on the programming of a completely different set of beliefs—like if my iPhone was running Android instead of iOS. It would *look* like an Apple product, but the way I actually go about running software is entirely informed by a Google system. No matter what your personal political beliefs, there is an excellent chance that you're running this neoliberal, individualist software.

And it's that software we use to program our goals. Journalist George Monbiot explains in an article for *The Guardian*, "Another paradox of neoliberalism is that universal competition relies upon universal quantification and comparison. The result is that workers, job-seekers and public services of every kind are subject to a pettifogging, stifling regime of assessment and monitoring, designed to identify the winners and punish the losers."[22] Goal-setting is one of the ways we manage ourselves—quotas, metrics, milestones. It's how we determine whether *we're* a winner or a loser. And we're terrified to be among the losers. But neoliberalism is simply the latest iteration of other political and personal philosophies that set the stage for our obsession. Before neoliberalism, there was Herbert Hoover's rugged individualism.

We'd Like to Thank You, Herbert Hoover

The decidedly romanticized idea of rugged individualism is perhaps the most influential philosophy of the U.S. social and political systems. Rugged individualism is a doctrine of self-reliance, an ethos that puts the responsibility for health, wealth, and general well-being on individual citizens and removes responsibility from society. This ethos is so engrained in the American mind that it can be difficult to imagine any other way to operate. Even those who vote for the most progressive policies are often pulled back into the spirit of rugged individualism in the way they run their own lives.

This is, of course, in part because the U.S. social and political systems necessitate that position. If you're not self-reliant, these systems will not help you—especially if you're a woman, a person of color, an LGBTQIA+ person, a disabled person, or an immigrant. There is no safety net, no helping hand, and few rules limiting exploitation. While

Hayek may argue that individualism doesn't constitute an ethos of selfishness, he does argue that people's concern should be on their own interests, their own "clearly delimited area of responsibility." We can see the direct impact of this reasoning on public health, tax policy, and funding for public programs. Hayek also asserted that, because "he cannot know more than a tiny part of the whole of society,"[23] he should only concern himself with immediate results of his actions on the tiny part he belongs to. While "eyes on your own paper" is a good rule for taking an exam, is it the rule we want to govern our communities? Hayek didn't preclude collaboration (as long as it doesn't involve "coercing" others), but he doesn't seem to be super interested in lending a hand if it's not in his best interests.

I believe this foundational individualism is a significant contributor to the epidemic of loneliness and disconnection. Late-stage self-reliance silos us off from the rest of the world, cutting off the ability to ask for and receive help from others. Individualism transforms us into hyper-vigilant self-managers when it comes to work, family, and life in general. In other words, the incessant emphasis on personal responsibility and self-reliance turns us into goal-setting machines.

On the surface, this ethos seems logical. If people are taking care of themselves, then everyone is taken care of, right? Except this absolutely does not work practically. In the speech in which soon-to-be President-Elect Herbert Hoover coined the phrase "rugged individualism," he triumphed the equality of opportunity and individual freedom that (he claimed) made America great. But it doesn't take a historian to realize that there were broad swathes of the U.S. citizenry that did *not* have equal access to opportunity or even individual freedom. Hoover was elected in the fever of the Jim Crow era and at the trailhead of the Great Depression. Women had gotten the vote just eight years prior. Most of the labor regulations—unequal as they were—and social safety net provisions were still seven years from being passed into law. Even Hoover recognized that rugged individualism shouldn't be an excuse for inequality or exploitation. He didn't want people to think that he was advocating for a "free-for-all and devil-take-the-hindmost" nation. "The very essence of equality of opportunity and of American individualism is that there shall be no domination by any group or [monopoly] in this republic," said Hoover.[24] Bold words from someone leading a nation under the spell of white industrialists, robber barons, and speculators.

The idea that American greatness was rooted in equal opportunity and individual freedom was, at best, laughable in 1928. And yet, it's a story that persists to this day. It's a story that informs the way people vote, the jobs they choose to train for, the way they manage their money, the family relationships they form, and—of course—influences the personal goals that they set. The story of rugged individualism is a fable, a tale that puts moral weight onto its central lesson: self-reliant, rugged, fiercely independent individuals are better people because of their doggedness. We set goals to survive or get ahead in this story— and doing so gives us some confidence in our inherent goodness and worthiness within society. But the moral component of our relationship to goals doesn't stop at the societal level, it continues into the spiritual realm.

Remember, Time Is Money

Before Hoover ever uttered the phrase *rugged individualism*, the United States was a nation that venerated self-discipline. In case your grasp of early American history has faded since elementary school (mine certainly has), remember that among the first colonists in what would become the United States were Puritans. Most of the people who traveled on the Mayflower and settled Plymouth Plantation were part of the Protestant separatist group seeking to get out from under the thumb of the Church of England. I'm going to get into the weeds of Christian theology a bit here but, as many sociologists have argued, these details are core to how we understand culture and economics in the United States. Bear with me. This is important.

Puritans, who were Calvinists, had some significant disagreements with the Church of England. The establishment of the Church of England as independent from the Roman Catholic Church was more about structures of power than it was theology. But Calvinists, like Lutherans, had a theological bone to pick with what had long been considered settled dogma. For Calvinists, one of the main disagreements was about justification—in other words, how one gets right with God and is ushered into salvation.

The Roman Catholic Church had long leaned on performing certain rituals as the method of justification. Baptism, mass, confession, last rites—these are all examples of sacraments that serve to purify the adherent. Martin Luther reformed this understanding of justification by calling out the ways in which the sacraments had been corrupted and used to exploit adherents throughout church history. Luther taught that God was the only source of justification—the individual's only role was in having faith in the sacrifice of Jesus on their behalf. But John Calvin took a slightly different stance on justification. While agreeing in principle with Luther, Calvin believed that justification took on a different quality among God's chosen people. He reasoned that because God was omnipotent, God already knew who was saved and who was damned. And that foreknowledge amounted to "predestination." The doctrine of predestination was simply that whether you were saved (a member of the Elect) or damned was determined before you were even born. There was nothing you could do in this life to impact your salvation.

Calvin maintained that one's status as Elect or not couldn't be known in this life. And, of course, that uncertainty was plenty to give believers an existential anxiety attack. So instead of working toward salvation through the sacraments or strengthening the faith by which you'd be saved, Calvinists started to look for evidence that they were among the Elect. One of the chief signs of salvation? Self-discipline. Those who were able to follow the rules, work hard, and improve their lot in life were thought to be the ones who could be confident in their future glory. And here is where we get an even more fundamental moral quality to hard work and self-improvement. Self-discipline, labor in a calling, and being a useful member of the community all served the purpose of glorifying God. Work is worship. Diligence is a ritual of faith. Puritanism was a distinctly individual experience, yet that experience created the foundations of highly structured and productive communities.

Sociologist and political economist Max Weber traced the connection between Protestant work ethic and capitalism in his aptly titled work, *Protestant Ethic and the Spirit of Capitalism*, back in 1904. He showed how anxiety over predestination increasingly became secularized in the form of capitalism. Weber frequently cited the essay in which Benjamin Franklin reminded his nephew, "time is money." Weber viewed this declaration as a sort of tipping point into a more purely economic construction of the Protestant work ethic. Weber writes: "The earning of money within the modern economic order is, so long as it is done legally, the result and the expression of virtue and proficiency in a calling; and this virtue and proficiency are, as it is now not difficult to see, the real Alpha and Omega of [Benjamin] Franklin's ethic."[25] Today, we can see how this secularization reversed itself as television evangelists preach the so-called prosperity gospel and religiously conservative politicians preach about the personal failings of the poor.

The legacy of Puritan culture—and other American Protestant sects, including the Anabaptists, Methodists, and Pietists—is the notion that not only are people who work hard, follow the rules, and improve themselves *morally good* people, they're saved from damnation. Rugged individualism and neoliberalism have translated this model of spiritual salvation into economic salvation. If I'm self-disciplined and, therefore, successful, it's a sign of my inherent goodness and relief from the eternal torture of poverty (or even working class status). Setting goals and New Year's resolutions have become a ritual of the doctrine of self-discipline. We pay penance by demonstrating our ability to control ourselves and delay gratification, proving ourselves worthy of economic and cultural salvation.

You Think You're Better Than Me?

No accounting of neoliberal or American culture in regards to our obsession with goals would be complete without an exploration of supremacy culture. In short, supremacy culture is made up of the norms and mores that result from believing one group is better than another group.[26] Multiple forms of supremacy have cropped up over the course of human history: men over women, white over Black, rich over poor, educated over uneducated, Global West over Global East, Global North over Global South, colonist over indigenous person. In the United States, we hear most about white (male) supremacy, but all of those hierarchies are embedded into our culture.

The construct of supremacy is key to our understanding of the role goals play in our lives because supremacy culture is what establishes "the ladder." The ladder, as writer and activist Sonya Renee Taylor described in an interview with Brené Brown, is the system by which we order who is better and who isn't as good.[27] To move up the ladder, you have to take on more traits of the groups who occupy status higher up the ladder. It's nice to think that the ladder is purely meritocratic—yet it's anything but. We don't move up the ladder because our work is better than the next person's or even because we've disciplined ourselves to achieve peak productivity. We move up the ladder because *better* and *more productive* are defined through the understanding of supremacy. What is white, Western, male, rich, educated, productive, and straight—or an approximation of those traits—is what moves up.

What that meant for me as a white woman from a working class family was that I needed to seek education, financial prosperity, and male-coded behaviors to move up the ladder. What it means for a mixed race transgender person is that they need to completely deny their identity in order to move up. Climbing the ladder requires self-erasure to one degree or another. The writer and spoken word artist Zuva Seven shared her own confrontation with the ladder in an essay for *An Injustice!* She wrote that it was her parents, immigrants to Great Britain from Zimbabwe, who made it clear that she needed to conform to succeed. "But success garnered from erasing myself isn't something I want. I don't want that to be what I am known for, nor do I want it to be my legacy," she wrote. For a time, she erased her own passion for writing, sexuality, and identity as a Black woman, opting to follow the success path her family laid out for her.[28]

Music, magazines, social media, work, school, family, and social groups can all impart the imperative to deny one's full identity and conform to the construct of supremacy is baked into how we set our goals. In *Country Living*'s list of "Top 10 New Year's Resolutions for 2022 Revealed," the first three pertain to body conformity, two pertain to financial conformity, and other five could best be described as ways to follow cultural commandments.[29] The result is that goals become a sort of technology for self-erasure. We learn to recognize all the ways we don't fit in and the rungs we haven't yet climbed and define our future selves against those traits. We rarely—if ever—stop to think whether the things we're *not* are actually a core part of who we *are*.

And that's not just a personal problem. It ripples out into our culture and communities, making them more hostile to difference.

Overcoming

Difference is something to be overcome—that's the prevailing message we receive through each of the narratives I've discussed in this chapter. Each presents a list of shoulds and supposed-tos that we can measure ourselves against to make "appropriate" adjustments. Not extroverted enough? Set a goal to become more outgoing. Not thin enough? Set a goal to stop eating sugar. Not rich enough? Set a goal to get started with a side hustle. Not male enough? Set a goal to be more assertive and aggressive. Not white enough? Set a goal to talk and dress the part. But overcoming differences doesn't work—at least not sustainably.

SPIRITUAL SALVATION

GOALS

ECONOMIC SALVATION   CULTURAL SALVATION

Ironing out your differences in order to conform inevitably leads to burnout or self-alienation, or both. It also takes up precious resources that could be better used on projects infinitely more meaningful to you. What would it take to view the differences we possess not as negative, not even as positive, but as … neutral? Facts rather than qualifiers. Circumstances rather than performance metrics. What works, in my opinion, is when we bring greater awareness to the systems we operate in and debug the code that guides how we think. The beautiful thing is that, as we debug our own code, we find ourselves in community with others, free from the competition and self-judgment we've taken on. And that community can act collectively to change the code at higher and higher levels. It might be an individual action at first, but the results are political and cultural.

What makes our obsession with goals so deeply rooted into our worldview is what also makes it so hard to divorce ourselves from. The goals we set represent a chance at a better life, a less challenging identity, even the hope of a sort of salvation. To give up goal-setting can feel like abandoning an imagined future self that has things a little easier. But at that point, I think we have to start to ask the question that evangelists of individualism, neoliberalism, Puritan work ethic, capitalism, and supremacy culture would rather us not ask: Why do we put up with all of these systems that make life so damn hard in the first place?

Even if we're done putting up with these systems as individuals, it will take time and work to dismantle them at higher levels. We can't stop at acceptance of our own differences. We have a duty to work toward new systems that allow people to accept their own differences— without the fear of harm, poverty, or the potential to become a social pariah. For now, though, we might think differently but we still need to cope with the way things are to a degree. Is there a way to operate within these foundational systems that allows us to get our own needs met while caring for others needs, too? Is there a stance we can take toward goal-setting, accomplishment, or ladder-climbing that doesn't rely on stepping over (or on) others?

My hope is that, through this brief exploration of rugged individualism, the doctrine of personal responsibility, Protestant work ethic, and supremacy culture, you notice the cultural narratives that shape what goals you perceive as worthy of pursuit and why those goals hold such massive influence over you. These narratives are deeply embedded in our worldview—if not your individual worldview, than the societal worldview. They shape our very identities. And so exploring identity is where we must go next.

Reflection:

- Which system is the most dominant in the way you make decisions today? How has that system impacted your goals or decisions?
- What aspects of who you are have you tried to overcome in order to conform to these systems? What was the result?
- What's your own understanding of the "rules" or code that you're supposed to follow? How does it differ from what I've shared here? How is it similar?

3

Who Am I without the Doing?

I was intrigued, as a child, that a bottle could also be a woman. She had a job, this woman, holding syrup. But when it was all poured out, when she was empty and her job was done, she became something else.
— Eula Biss, *Having and Being Had*[30]

I USED TO love personality tests. Myers-Briggs was a bit of a hobby of mine for a while (I'm an INTP: introverted, intuitive, thinking, prospecting). I was certified to consult on the Fascination Advantage system (Maestro). I introduced my clients to the Enneagram (Type 3). I've worked with the Big Five, StrengthsFinder, and the Via Character Strengths Assessment. Give me a computer screen full of multiple-choice questions and the possibility of a new insight into who I am or what I'm about, and I'll happily click "strongly agree" or "very unlike me" all day long.

After learning that I'm autistic—which did kick off with multiple-choice assessment after assessment—I started to rethink these tests. Take a simple question from a Big Five assessment: "I don't talk a lot." Agree, neutral, or disagree? That's a big fat "depends" for me. A big part of my work is podcasting—literally talking into a microphone a lot. But on the other hand, in a group of strangers, I will absolutely not

47

talk unless I have to. If I'm talking about one of my revolving special interests, it's hard to shut me up. I've had to learn to look for when someone's eyes glaze over to cue me to wrap it up. But on the other hand, if I have more than one or two meetings in a day, I won't be able to carry on a conversation with my husband. And there are times when I experience a "shut down" from overstimulation that renders me mute.

Personality profiles give us a framework for understanding ourselves. But they're not designed to tolerate much real difference. Functionally, if not purposely, they often work to train us toward change (i.e., personality improvement) or to cope with our deficits. As I process my autism diagnosis, I want to accept and integrate the differences innate to my identity. My differences were things I worked to change for so long, trying to overcome the ways that they held me back from greater success and achievement. For instance, on the Via Character Strengths Assessment, my lowest rated trait is—wait for it—*love*. The way I experience loving relationships will always be different than other people. I'm never going to be the kind of person who has multiple close friends and a circle of pals whom I socialize with regularly. I will never be the kind of person who uses physical affection or even affectionate words with anyone other than my daughter and husband. If those are the ways you measure my capacity for love, well, sure, I'm going to score low. But that doesn't mean I live a loveless life. It doesn't mean I'm unfulfilled or unhappy when it comes to relationships. It's just the way I'm wired.

We all have characteristics that make us different. I grew up in the 1980s and 1990s so I got that message in an intravenous drip. Often, those differences are central to our many identities and how we understand ourselves. And at the same time, those differences are often the very things that we end up trying to change in order to conform. We try to overcome those differences instead of working with them. We labor to subdue those differences to become a better fit for the workplace, our families, or our communities. But as we do, we reinforce our suspicion that we don't belong or aren't good enough, making it difficult to accept our identities for what they are. While it will always take some adaptation to live and work together, there has to be a balance. We can't always sacrifice our differences and our identities in order to please those whose identities aren't perceived as different (e.g., white, straight, male, cis, upper-middle class). In an effort to find my own balance, I've learned to pay attention to when I'm adapting—or being asked to adapt—and negotiate for time and space to let my differences breathe. I need to be comfortable with my own identities so that I know when I'm compromising any one of them. I can't say that I'm close to fully processing what autism means for my identity and how I operate in the world. But I can say that becoming more familiar with that identity has made me less motivated to change my personality than I once was. I'm marginally more accepting of Who I Am. It's been a long road and taken a lot of work, though. Work that started years before learning I'm autistic. It's work that started with a question: Who are you without the doing?

I first heard that question in the middle of a workout while listening to the *Hurry Slowly* podcast. I was in my favorite spot in the gym—easy access to everything, but isolated and out of the way. I can still feel the rough texture of the gym's beaten up exercise mat under my fingertips as I listened to host Jocelyn K. Glei explain that a healer had posed that question to her: Who are you without the doing? Glei shared that she was trying to find the answer.[31] I certainly didn't have an answer for myself. I wasn't even sure I could understand the premise of the question. It certainly derailed my workout—and the rest of that day. In many ways, that question spawned each of the other questions that make up this book. I had to find the answer—who *am* I without the doing? This question led me to exploring the nature of identity. I needed to know whether there was something innately "me" underneath all of my pursuits and accomplishments. I want to be clear: This chapter does *not* propose an answer to this question. I still can't describe an innately "me" identity—but trying to figure it out has been its own reward.

Who Am I?

Think about the last time you were asked to introduce yourself to a group. Maybe it was a new group of co-workers, some classmates, or a social group. If it happened recently, your eyes probably darted between the tiny black circle of your webcam and the window that held faces displayed from odd angles. If it was in person, maybe each member of the group sat, slightly nervous and fidgeting, while you stood to rattle off some biological details. What did you choose to say? Why did you go with that answer? As a facilitator, I've often had the surprisingly difficult job of leading a group of strangers through introductions like these. It seems like it should be easy enough, right? I might say, "Tell everyone who you are and where you're calling from." But from there, things can get wild. One person might introduce themselves using their first name, occupation, and physical location. Another person might use their full name, a bit of personal history, current interests, and which room of the house they're in. And still another person might introduce themselves in relation to others (wife, dad, manager), their current project, and acknowledgement of the stolen land they occupy. Some people might take 30 seconds for their introduction while others take five minutes. Some will be self-assured, and others will be looking for approval from the group.

The way these introductions play out tells us a lot about the assumptions that are present in the group. If it's a work function, like a networking group, there is probably an assumption that title or occupation is an important identity to include in an introduction. If it's a parenting group, there is probably an assumption that including your relationship to your child is an important identity to include. But there are almost always outliers, too. There are people who prioritize other identities and view themselves in different ways than what might be expected. That reveals a lot too. Still thinking of that last time you had to introduce yourself? Consider how your introduction revealed the assumptions you made about how you fit into the group as well as what it revealed about your values and relationships. The varied ways we can introduce ourselves expose one of the key challenges to answering a question like "Who am I without the doing?" Who Am I is relational, situational, and multidimensional. There is no one essential way to answer that question.

Philosopher Kathleen Wallace proposes that we consider the self as a network. Other theories of self have had more of an essentialist quality; our identity is the psychological continuity we experience from birth to death or the simple fact of being a human biological organism. These two frameworks position the self as being contained within the body—either as the mind or our life-sustaining functions. Wallace explains that both of these frameworks are trying to get to the *essence*—the singular quality—of self. We can feel the shortcoming with that singular approach to self every time we get asked to introduce ourselves. On the other hand, Wallace's approach—what she calls "the network self"—is inclusive of multiple identities. Instead of expecting the self to be singular, even immutable, the network self theory creates the space for the ways we think of ourselves differently depending on context. Wallace accepts that the body and mind are key parts of the self but so are relationships—whether to communities, to social categories, or to other individuals. As those relationships change over time, so do those aspects of our identities.[32] For instance, I haven't always been a wife or mother. But when I entered into those relationships, my identity shifted. I had a new self that influenced my other identities. Similarly, I spent 38 years thinking I was just a hardcore introvert with mental health challenges. When I learned that I am autistic, that aspect of self took on a new quality.

Wallace's approach makes a lot of sense to me. While things that I *do* certainly make up my network self (things like running, writing, or podcasting), they are not the *only* thing that makes up my network self. When I map my own network self, I see evidence of the multidimensionality of Who I Am. I can start to wrap my head around how I am both Who I Am when I was 8, or 12, or 22 years old—while also being distinctly different. At those ages, I wasn't a mother, a wife, or a divorcé. I wasn't a business owner, a writer, or a runner. Yet those are all key components of Who I Am now and how I conceive of the potential for my self to continue to evolve, as are the identities I held at 8, 12, or 22 that I no longer hold now.

Without the Doing

Exploring identity is key to exploring our relationship to goals. Goals are one way we've learned to express our identities or work toward a new identity. What we decide to do—the goals we pursue, the accomplishments we work for—is a way of either expressing how we understand an aspect of ourselves or an identity that will give us more power within existing systems. Both forms of expression can cause problems. For instance, self-delusion can lead us to pursue activities that don't actually line up with our authentic network self. Or, we can choose objectives that alienate parts of our identity in order to climb the ladder.

It's the latter that I'm most concerned with here. The mistakes—if we can call them that—we make as a result of self-delusion or a lack of self-awareness can certainly cause pain. But they also often lead to new knowledge and understanding. They become stepping stones on the path to self-actualization. But when what we do ends up alienating parts of our identities (maybe gender, race, disability, sexuality), we end up clinging to those actions because we've lost the tether to ourselves.

Psychologist and psychoanalyst Paul Veraeghe argues that our identities are transformed by the systems we operate within—represented by the market. The reason we feel such pressure to manage and discipline ourselves is because that's what the market requires of us. We seek new identities in order to increase our market value. The relationships formed within the market are mediated through our ability to overcome difference and climb the ladder toward greater power. Education, parenting, career development, even hobbies—they're all seen in economic terms. Veraeghe positions our contemporary Western understanding of identity squarely within the context of the neoliberal meritocratic environment. Our identities, therefore, are perceived within the genealogy of cultural systems explored in Chapter 2: supremacy culture, Protestant work ethic, and rugged individualism. Who we believe we are is based on what we do to climb the ladder. Or as Veraeghe puts it, "The individual's new identity as entrepreneur goes hand in hand with a new life goal: success. Success is something to be aimed for all the time—not just in exams, but also on holiday, in relationships, and in the workplace."[33]

On the Internet

To separate Who I Am from What I Do, we have to understand how much our identities are wrapped up in this broader social and economic context. This is only made more difficult by the technology we use to curate and amplify our identities today—technology that is largely used to signal our self-management, entrepreneurship, and market value. For many people, it's not enough to toil away at perfecting our market-based identities in the privacy of our own homes or cubicles. We feel compelled to broadcast that work on Instagram or TikTok. I'll admit here that I'm personally a bit torn on this.

Without broadcasting my work (both personal and professional) on Instagram or via my email newsletter, I would not be writing this book right now. I wouldn't have an audience of people who were interested in the things I think about or the experience I have to share with them. And in all transparency, I've intentionally pursued experiences that would "look good" on Instagram that have turned into truly meaningful additions to my life. But I also can't deny that any sense of "freedom" I have about what I post or how I share details of my life is an illusion. Just like in any quantified environment, I am heavily influenced by what is measured and who (or what) is doing the measuring. This influence drastically increases the likelihood that I'll select goals that "perform well" on social media (I explore why in Chapter 6). While I'm not always conscious of it, I look for a way to signal something about *me* that will connect with *you*. And unlike in a conversation where there is mutual exchange by which to evaluate the quality of that connection, on the internet, I have cold hard metrics. I know what I need to signal about myself by the likes and shares that signaling receives. This might not be how everyone uses the internet or social media. But the omnipresence of metrics certainly influences the way we relate to ourselves and others.

There's a line from Jia Tolentino's *Trick Mirror* that hits uncomfortably close to home for me: "On the internet, a highly functional person is one who can promise everything to an indefinitely increasing audience at all times."[34] I'm old enough to remember a time when "on the internet" would have been a qualifying phrase that aptly applied to just time spent online. But I'm also young enough that I've never known a professional life that wasn't molded by what happens "on the internet." We've integrated the experience of the internet so deeply that the influence of likes and shares is bound to bleed over in "real life." Your goals represent the promises you make to "your audience." That audience might be your manager and coworkers, or it might be the audience that you're actively cultivating online, or it might even be your family and friends. These promises aren't necessarily bad, but they're not necessarily virtuous either. A promise might influence my behavior in a way that's meaningful to me, but it just as easily might influence me to conform to meritocratic norms that don't serve my well-being or contribution to society. What's more, as our actions are influenced by what Richard Seymour dubs the twittering machine, our identities are revealed to us by the algorithm.[35] Not only does the machine tell us who we are and who we will become, it turns around and sells us the symbols of this identity. My identity is commodified in an instant. Who I Am and What I Do On the Internet can feel like an act of self-expression, but they are more likely artifacts of conformity.

We can see this in stark display within the so-called creator economy. The promise of the creator economy is that, as an amateur individual, you can follow your passion and create content (e.g., photos, videos, writing, podcasts) that builds an audience and, eventually, creates a livelihood by leveraging platform technologies (e.g., Instagram, Substack, TikTok, etc. . . .). It's the classic "Do what you love and you'll never work a day in your life" grift. In a survey by the research firm Nonfiction, 93 percent of respondents indicated that becoming a creator has had a *negative* impact on their lives. Why? Well, one reason is likely another data point on the survey: "70 percent say that a dip in earnings from an algorithm change could have 'serious effects' on their life. Looking at these findings, it's no wonder that 33 percent have felt anger, rage, or extreme frustration with major social media platforms as they navigate this uncertainty."[36]

Creators are basing their livelihoods on the performance of an identity through the expression of their knowledge, experiences, or talents. This performance is a sort of funhouse-mirror version of how professionals and the upwardly mobile have performed their identity for decades. The more the algorithm influences what creators decide to produce, the more it distends their sense of self. They decide on goals and projects to satisfy the current whims of the platform—and have to change course as soon as the platform decides to prioritize a new type of content or user engagement metric. Rebecca Jennings, who covers internet culture for *Vox*, has observed the consequences among TikTokers she's spoken with. They're driven to mold themselves into something "solidly monetizable" to maintain the fame that's become the basis of their livelihoods. Jennings writes, "They seamlessly toggle between their two identities—the real person and the online persona—and speak with a kind of cynicism about tying their livelihoods to a platform that could disappear in an instant. It all feels like stuff they shouldn't have to think about, not yet."[37]

The algorithm determines what users see. That means the algorithm also effectively determines what users *create* too because you can't generate income if no one is seeing your content. Yet, the algorithms that platforms like Instagram and TikTok use are always changing—and they're always changing in order to generate more ad money for the owners of the platforms. These platforms have no vested interest in the success of individual creators, of course. They're invested in building a space in which enough people create what consumers want to see. The platforms need consumers to spend copious amounts of time scrolling through content because that's how these platforms generate profit.

We can extrapolate this out into the broader economy and the way we conform to whatever "platform" influences the way we perform our labor. I think of conforming to the requirements of high school and then college, the standards of my first full-time job, and the expectations of entrepreneurship. The incentive structure of our educators, employers, or clients influences our behavior and how we understand our value to their enterprise. If teaching to the test will result in appearing more successful as an educator, then that's what educators will do. At the same time, students learn in a way that optimizes for test-taking. If employers are incentivized to reduce expenses, that's what our employers will do. And workers learn that they're most valuable when they cost the company the very least.

I think many—if not most—of us have experienced this in how we assimilate to a work environments. Even outside of particular performance expectations, every work environment has cultural expectations. *Professionalism* is a code word for one set of expectations—a construct of supremacy culture. *Passion* is another code word for a set of expectations—an evolution of the Protestant work ethic and the moral good of laboring in one's vocation. Efficiency and productivity are typically part of these cultural expectations, too. But even aside from these more wide-reaching norms, individual workplaces have idiosyncratic cultural expectations.

For instance, I spoke at Etsy headquarters during its initial growth period. At that time, Etsy was located exactly where you'd expect it to be located—in the Dumbo area of Brooklyn in a converted brick factory building. The office was full of people who clearly had better taste than I did—albeit in a quirky, vintage, Brooklyn-esque way. When I traveled there, I was extremely intentional about what I wore so that I had even the slightest chance of fitting in. I never did, and I always felt a little out of place regardless of how welcoming everyone was. Even when I managed the bookstore after college, I felt the pull to assimilate to our workplace culture. There, my co-workers all seemed so worldly—privy to musicians, authors, and films that I had no knowledge of. One co-worker obsessed on British pop punk, another obsessed on manga. I had my own obsessions at the time—contemporary Christian theology and science fiction—but they never felt like the way to really plug into our work culture.

The truth is that I fit into both of those environments more than I realized at the time. I might not have gotten the costume or the script quite right, but I was still playing my part well. But could I get even more into character? Certainly, my relationship to these work cultures influenced the goals I set and the ways I sought to grow. And my intention here isn't to suggest that that is somehow wrong or bad, just to observe the influence—and pose questions about whether our goals are our own or the result of the work we do to fit in and optimize our standing in the work environment—whether that's to performance metrics or to the latest hipster glasses trend.

Our success is not objective but relative to the decisions of those who hold the power. So as long as my identity hinges on What I Do, I'll set goals that optimize my performance accordingly. Now, I can imagine people reading—maybe you—who are ready to argue on this point. They set goals in opposition, in resistance, to the capitalist and meritocratic systems they participate in. Maybe then you find your identity in What You Don't Do. A relationship based on opposition is a relationship nonetheless. Your goals are still being influenced by the context of our culture.

Acknowledging the influence of external forces on our identities isn't all that different from recognizing that algorithms influence what you decide to post or share on social platforms. The question of how we navigate that influence—what parts of it we consciously use and which parts we discard—is key to the development of our sense of self. Exploring that question gives us a basis for pursuing what matters rather than setting goals based on what others deem good or productive.

Who Am I Becoming?

One of my favorite questions—and one that I'll ask you to answer for yourself later on—is: Who am I becoming? Whether we talk about precise targets, personal projects, or new habits, any change in our behavior will impact our sense of self in some way. By imagining that future sense of self, we can better evaluate whether what we might pursue is really what we want to pursue. This question also helps us identify stories, assumptions, and beliefs that make it infinitely harder to grow or change. Before we get into how we can use this question, though, let's look at the question itself.

While there are a number of fairly complementary theories of psychological development, I want to focus on one, that of developmental psychologist Robert Kegan. Kegan combines two modes of human psychology—constructivism and developmentalism—to create his theory of constructive development theory. Constructivism is the theory that we construct our own sense of reality and meaning as agents in the world. What we perceive isn't some objective, scientifically knowable thing. Our perception of what's "out there" is always a formulation of our cumulative knowledge and experience. Developmentalism, on the other hand, is the idea that we grow not only physically but psychologically as we get older. Originally, this development was thought to occur through infancy, childhood, and adolescence—with people over the age of 20 or so being "completed" psychologically speaking, much like we stop getting taller around puberty. But Kegan and others have demonstrated that psychological development can occur over a lifetime.[38]

In combining these two schools of thought, Kegan constructs five orders of psychological development. The first two orders, the Impulsive Mind and the Instrumental Mind, you might think of as an "immature" mind. In these phases of development, we are at the whim of our material needs or individual concerns. In the third order of development, what Kegan calls the Socialized Mind, we begin to understand that others have their *own* material needs and individual concerns. We start to construct our relationship to the world as a relationship with others. We seek to better understand their values and positions not merely so we can figure out whether they can meet our needs but so that we can live together. We start to internalize the values of our community so that they become our values, too. We make judgments based on the thinking, "People like me do things like this." This is the post-adolescent mind—the one that makes you "reliable" and "trustworthy," according to Kegan.

The fourth order of development is the Self-Authoring Mind. During this phase, we gain distance from the values of our community so that we have more personal authorship over our own opinions and identity. We don't shrug off the values of our community, necessarily. We can just see them for what they are and make a more intentional decision to uphold them or deviate from them. Instead of using the idea "people like me do things like this" as a road map for how to behave (or what goals to set), we can see that, yes, "some people like me do things like this *and* other people do things differently." We can choose to self-author by trying out the behavior of other groups or individuals based on our own sense of authority and intention. In other words, we ask questions that start to resemble, "Who am I becoming?"

Finally, the fifth order of development is the Self-Transforming Mind. This phase, which many adults never enter into, is defined by its ability to see one's own sense of authority at a distance. The personal values, identity, and relationships that the Self-Authoring Mind has been based on can be changed, built upon. I believe "Who Am I Becoming" is a question for the Self-Transforming Mind. To decide who you want to become requires a self-awareness that can not only perceive agency in how you construct your values and identity but the potential to grow toward new or evolved values and identity based on new information.

Today, most goal-setting advice published in the United States is directed to the socialized mind (Kegan's third order), maybe the self-authoring mind (fourth order). Goal-setting advice encourages us toward growth, productivity, and achievement. It instructs us on how to work harder and get ahead. And, of course, it fills our heads with positive affirmations and personal responsibility. In other words, goal-setting advice is building on the shared moral framework of neoliberal meritocracy. The problem? Neoliberalism serves the already powerful, while our systems of power are anything but meritocratic. We plod away as cogs in the wheel of a system designed to make us better and better consumers instead of creating real opportunities for self-actualization. One might even say that neoliberal meritocracy is an objectifying system intended to remove our agency and bend us to its will.

Objectification is the process by which a subject—an entity with the ability to act upon an object—is rendered powerless, reduced to a mere object. The subject-object dichotomy is key concept of philosophy that has been built upon over generations. The idea is simply that some entities—for our purposes, *humans*—have the agency to decide for themselves what action they will take, what resources they will use, and what end they will work toward; these are subjects. Objects, on the other hand, become the tools of subjects. They're reduced to their ability to fulfill the needs of subjects. You're likely already familiar with this idea in terms of sexual objectification. A human—most often a woman—is reduced to her body as a tool for providing a subject—most often a man—pleasure (or at least, arousal).

My argument is that most of us have experienced a similar objectification via our culture and economy. The goals we set assume a certain level of buy-in to the system that begs us to strive for the promotion, eke out a 2 percent increase in a key performance indicator, or ensure that our children never get more than the recommended allotment of screen time per day. The system commodifies our labor and colonizes our time with the intended outcome being that we achieve more on the job so that we can consume more at home. We've become tools for economic growth rather than agents who get to make choices based on their own moral guidance and authority. Or as journalists Anne Helen Petersen and Charlie Warzel put it, "Too many people who work hard and strive for success self-objectify as excellent work machines and tools of performance."[39]

The COVID-19 pandemic brought this into stark clarity. Grocery store clerks, warehouse workers, and food delivery drivers were objectified under the umbrella of "essential workers." They were valorized for allowing consumers to keep on consuming. As the pandemic has worn on, objectified workers were assumed to be lazy and unpatriotic for not returning to unsafe work environments, finding a magical solution to the childcare crisis, or wanting to be screamed at by people who were irate about public health policies. Emergency support—increased unemployment benefits, hazard pay, safety measures—ceased as an "incentive" to get back to normal well before the pandemic ended. At the same time, consumers were urged to keep buying, to "support local restaurants," and to "shop local." Our patriotic duty was (and had been) to spend money. As citizens, we were objectified as tools of a consumer economy. The stimulus checks that were issued weren't relief—at least not toward the economic stress on citizens. Those checks were designed to relieve the stress on the economy. Relief that was geared to citizens would have been channeled into mortgage or rent help—rather than deferral of payment. It would have included free masks delivered to every household (before March 2022). No, that extra $2,000 was designed to be channeled right back into the economy in the form of home improvements, vacations, and takeout.

Maybe you were one of those objectified workers. Or maybe you've been the objectified consumer. (Or both!) The vast majority of us have some experience of objectification at the hands of the culture and economy we live in. That objectification absolutely extends to the goals we set and the options we consider for growth. Why go for that promotion? Well, I'll make more money and get to consume more—life will be easier. Why go to college? I'll get a better job and feel more stable. Why exercise daily? I'll be healthier (read: be a better consumer of healthcare), and I'll lose weight so that I'll have more opportunities for me at work and in romance. Okay, I realize this is a really cynical view of the reason we set goals. I recognize that, for most of us, we're not conscious of the conditioning that leads us to set the goals that we set. And, there is genuine desire behind many of the goals we set. You might want a promotion because you crave a greater challenge—the raise is just a bonus. Or you want to go to college because you love to learn, and you want the chance to really dive into one of your favorite subjects. Maybe you want to exercise daily because it's pleasurable.

Really, I'm not anti-goal-setting. I'm anti-objectification. I believe that the ways we've been sold on goals, planning, and productivity is just another way to turn us into better cogs in the machine. And I believe that, by shifting the way we set goals and organize our lives, we can reclaim our agency—and become self-transforming subjects who live lives that are meaningful and purposeful based on our own values and priorities.

Reflection:

- What traits, relationships, and identities make up your network self? In what ways you do shift between them on a daily or weekly basis?
- What identities do you try to hide or overcome to become more successful?
- How does the last goal you set reflect an aspect of your identity? How does it reflect an aspect of the systems you operate in?

4

The Satisfaction of Practice in an Achievement-Oriented World

*The rules had been constructed long before I was born, and I did not know yet
I was allowed to break them or redefine them or ignore them entirely.*
— Jami Attenberg, *I Came All
This Way to Meet You*[40]

THANKS TO MY daughter's persistent recommendation of a particular
digital art app, I started drawing in early 2021. Visual art has never
been an aspiration of mine. My brother is a talented artist, and anything
I tried to create paled in comparison to his effortless renderings. And
goodness knows I don't like to play second fiddle. But sketching on my
iPad while watching YouTube or bingeing old television shows in the
evening became a way to calm my mind as I went through a particularly
difficult mental health year.

At first, I played with color and textures—nonrepresentational art.
Then, I followed step-by-step tutorials to recreate images. Eventually,
I gave myself the go-ahead to fly solo. Instead of relying on someone's
detailed instructions, I would find an image I liked and break it down
into shapes and proportions that I could recreate. It's been slow yet

rewarding work. This drawing practice has also been a study in finding satisfaction with imperfection and inadequacy as well as joy in the process rather than in accomplishment. I've probably created a thousand or more images in a thousand or more hours. None of them will make me any money or win me any accolades. Not so long ago, I would not have devoted that much time to something with such middling results. But the results are only middling if the purpose of the time I spend drawing is to achieve a great (or marketable) piece of art. The purpose of this time, though, is not achievement. It's practice—a practice that relieves anxiety, stretches my self-imposed restrictions, and nurtures a deep sense of satisfaction.

For most of my life, I'd avoid anything that didn't come easily to me. If I tried a new activity and didn't get better-than-average results in short order, I simply wouldn't do that activity again. My identity was wrapped up in being a person who is good at things. If I wasn't good at something, I couldn't do it and retain that identity. As I got older, I realized how much I limited myself, how many incredible experiences I denied myself. Because I like to win, I tend to choose activities that give me a greater chance of winning. Because I like for things to come easily to me, I avoid experiences that I might have to work at to enjoy. It's hard to learn new things when you only do things you're already good at, you know?

One thing that I'm really good at, however, is routine. Once I've established a routine, I'm unlikely to deviate from it. It's one of my autistic superpowers. So when I decided to change up things and stretch myself, I knew I needed to establish a routine. I started slowly—setting an alarm instead of waking up on my own, a privilege that I enjoyed ever since I became self-employed. Once up, I powered up the treadmill and took a 10-minute walk. Ten minutes became 15 minutes, 15 minutes became 20 minutes, and the dead of winter became the dawn of spring. With the temperature a bit warmer and my energy a bit higher, I started jogging. I picked up other exercise activities that I was curious about along the way: powerlifting, hiking, bouldering, yoga. It was all new to me. And I wasn't good at any of it to start. In some of these pursuits, I did improve over time, and I certainly trained my body to withstand more demand. But I discovered what I really loved about these new additions to my routine was how they made me feel while

I did them. Even when I earned a medal after a race or sent a difficult boulder problem, I found that what was really meaningful to me in the experience was knowing how I'd put in the work. I felt good about what had gotten me to that point of relative excellence, rather than just finding meaning in the outcome of my work.

I'd stumbled on something that Kieran Setiya describes in his book, *Midlife: A Philosophical Guide*, as the difference between telic and atelic activities. In philosophy, teleology is the pursuit of understanding the goals or purposes of things. *Telos* is a Greek word that Aristotle uses to describe an entity's full purposes or ultimate end goal. In a metaphysical sense, that might be the greater purpose of one's life or the goal of their belief system. But for our purposes, I want to examine this idea of *telos* and, as Setiya puts it, telic activities, in a much more mundane way. Let's start with one of the core reasons that our goals make us miserable: the fact that they're designed to end. Setiya states it clearly:

> Think of it this way. What gives purpose to your life is having goals. Yet in pursuing them, you either fail (not good) or in succeeding, bring them to a close. If what you care about is achievement— earning a promotion, having a child, writing a book, saving a life— the completion of your project may be of value, but it means that the project can no longer be your guide.[41]

So far, I've focused on why the goals we set make us miserable. I've examined the moral systems they derive from and the objectifying forces that compel us to set many of the most common types of goals. I've considered how we seek greater power through our goals and perpetuate systems of harm in the process. But here, we look at goal-setting as a problem in and of itself. Setiya defines telic activities as being those focused on their end goals. A telic activity might be the task of making dinner, accomplishment of completing a work project, or achievement of running a marathon; worthwhile activities, to be sure. But once they end, we're at a loss for what is next, or we realize that we'll just do the same thing tomorrow. When we organize our lives around this relentless cycle of completion, we risk the sort of going-through-the-motion malaise that leads to many career and family crises. Setiya contrasts telic activities with atelic activities—those activities in which value is found through doing them rather than in completing them. Atelic activities might be taking a walk or playing music with friends. It's not that they don't eventually end—it's just that completion isn't the point of the activity.

As a culture, we obsess on telic activities. We believe that, each time we accomplish a task, we climb that old familiar ladder. When really, we're just putting miles on the treadmill (shout out to the runners who enjoy the treadmill, I am not one of those people). We set goals, create plans, and we strive toward their completion—in lock step with a whole industry that promotes this as the key to living a good life. Setiya argues that, while there is value in planning projects or working toward particular outcomes, our over-reliance on telic activities and end goals keeps us fixated on the future, ignoring the meaning of the present moment.

For me, and for Setiya, telic and atelic activities can have considerable overlap. And switching one's orientation from future outcomes to present mindfulness can have a huge impact on overall satisfaction (a concept I'll explore soon). It's here that I want to abandon this philosophical jargon—as fun for me as it might be—to offer up two more familiar terms to describe what Setiya is getting at: *achievement* and *practice*.

I prefer these terms because they help to describe how an outcome-oriented activity can be recast as a process with value in and of itself. For instance, I'm writing this chapter on New Year's Eve—the day before many people will attempt to "get healthy" and take up running. I'll see them out on the trail tomorrow, huffing and puffing. And good for them! But here's the thing, for many, they'll define *get healthy* as losing some weight. For them, running is a means to an end—it isn't a meaningful activity in and of itself. Others might set the goal of running a springtime 5K or half-marathon. Once the race is over, will they stick with running? Some will, but many will not. Running might accomplish the "achievement" of losing those pesky 10 pounds or completing the race, but it won't become a part of daily life for many of the people who decide to take it up tomorrow. At the risk of sounding self-congratulatory, the reason I've been able to stick with exercising every morning for five years is because I've embraced the practice. I find value in the time I spend pounding the pavement or on the yoga mat.

This shift doesn't only apply to exercise, of course. Cleaning the house might feel like a chore that has value only once it's finished. What would it take to turn cleaning into a process that provides value in doing it? For me, the answer is extra time to listen to podcasts. Completing a report at work might feel like busywork—something that only seems to have value because someone has required you to do it. What would it take to turn the process of completing that report into a satisfying process? Maybe you make a habit of hitting play on a favorite album each time you do that report. Or maybe you use the report as an opportunity to thank each member of your team for their particular contribution to the work that week. There will always be tasks or required outcomes that can't be turned into a satisfying process. And certainly, privilege is a big component into how successfully you convert chores into satisfying activities. But reconceiving much of how you spend your time into practice is absolutely possible.

What Is *Practice*?

Okay, so what do I mean by *practice*? First, I absolutely, positively do not mean "practice makes perfect." The purpose of practice is not perfection, or even improvement. The purpose of practice is presence, groundedness, and perspective. Practice can be extremely simple—no equipment or software needed—and transform basic activities into something nourishing or satisfying.

As I mentioned earlier, routines are one of my autistic superpowers. Autistic people often develop routines that help them navigate the world and their emotions. My routines are extremely important to me. I don't do them compulsively, but I do feel off when I haven't gone through an important routine. For example, my morning routine consists of a cup of Aeropress coffee, a big bowl of nondairy Greek yogurt with fruit and cereal, time with whatever book I'm reading, and then my workout for the day, which ideally ends with a long walk listening to one of my favorite podcasts. I wake up between 5:00 a.m. and 5:30 a.m. every weekday morning in order to move through that three-hour routine before I start work, and I've been doing it for well over three years. When we visit my husband's family in Montana, I don't have access to all the same "ingredients" of my routine. But

I recreate it as best as I can. I brew my coffee in the Keurig, eat a different brand of nondairy yogurt, and read my book. Then I drive myself somewhere I can get in a good long walk and listen to a podcast. The same thing goes if I'm traveling for work or on vacation. I know it probably sounds like a burden, but it's grounding.

My morning routine is a practice. It's something I come to every day to find presence and perspective. When I don't want to get out of bed, I think about how good I'll feel eating my yogurt and drinking my coffee. When I know I have a busy day full of difficult tasks, I linger in that routine to saturate myself with everything it has to offer me. Practice shows up in my life in plenty of other ways, too. Writing is practice; baking is practice; podcasting is practice; reading is practice. They are activities that remind me where I am and offer me space for observing my own thoughts and feelings, even though each of these activities result in tangible outcome. The essay, loaf of bread, episode, or completed book aren't the point of these activities. They're the byproduct of time spent mindfully.

The way I engage practice is no doubt privileged. But there are so many ways to incorporate practice into daily life, small ways to turn the mundane into the satisfying. Maybe you take the bus to work, and you find that walking to the bus stop shifts your mood when you listen to music—that's practice. Maybe you feed your cats, as I do, at the same time every evening, and you use that small amount of time to watch how their little bodies move eagerly while they wait—that's practice.

My guess is that I'm not telling you something you don't already know. #savorthemoment, amirite? Yet, when we make practice intentional and conscious, we shift our relationships to systems of power. These systems would rather keep us rushing around, constantly consuming, and producing more and more with our time. Practice is resistance. It reduces urgency, creates satisfaction, and reminds you that there is more to life than being productive. I don't think it's going too far to say that practice is a good way to "stick it to the man."

Thinking Interdependently

Let's set aside systems of power for a bit and examine *systems thinking*. Systems thinking is also practice. When we think in systems, we prioritize the interconnection of inputs and outputs—all the components that make up a beautifully messy system. Often, when we set a goal or make a plan, we focus on a particular outcome. We treat the goal as if it can be met by checking items off a list. But this thinking blurs the fact that to achieve or create anything, we come into contact with other processes and lists. Systems thinking reminds us that everything is connected. Sharon Salzberg writes about this in her book *Real Change*: "A change to one element affects the entire system. From this vantage point, interdependence is seen as the very fabric of every experience. A systems approach tends to focus on the relationships, structures, and feedback loops that make up the whole. That way we are constantly learning, seeing the problem as an ever-changing process."[42] Salzberg's thinking about systems echoes the work of Donella Meadows, a leading environmental and systems thinker of the 20th century. Meadows describes the world as "nonlinear, turbulent, and chaotic." Embracing systems thinking, she argues, is to work *with* that turbulence rather than against it.[43] The dynamism that surrounds us creates an incredible learning opportunity. But if we're constantly struggling to make the world—or at least our tiny corner of it—more static by squeezing it into our specific goals and linear plans, we end up frustrated, miserable, and often without the satisfaction of experiencing something new.

At least in the Western world, we're taught to organize our lives around achievement. Not necessarily the merit badge or trophy kind of achievement. It might be the achievement of getting dinner on the table in 30 minutes or less or making sure to file all the correct reports each week. It is this kind of achievement that breeds the sort of anxiety and angst that builds over the course of an adult life. We are instructed to "stick with" our goals, our plans, our resolutions. And we relentlessly evaluate ourselves to figure out how to do better. Yet, there seems to be no end to this struggle. Sure, I've gotten dinner on the table again, against all odds, but I just have to do it again tomorrow. I've filed all the correct reports this week, but I'll just have to do it again next week. There is a relatively satisfying practice to be found in each activity, yet our planners and to-do lists are all configured to the completion of the task rather than the *doing* of the task. We can even see this achievement-oriented, anxiety-inducing treadmill in our productivity advice: how to get more *done* in less time. It seems that we exist to complete tasks rather than to experience our connection to the wider world.

Salzberg, describing meditation practice, explains that practice allows us to rediscover our agency, our full range of options for action, and our values. And it's from this position that I've reclaimed my own connection to the world around me, unimpeded by the isolation of never-ending to-do lists or the seeming inevitability of the next "right" action. Every activity that I practice—writing, reading, walking, running, baking, grocery shopping—brings me back into the present. Practice creates an anchor in the chaotic world that Meadows describes.

My husband is one of the most practice-oriented people I've ever met. First, he's a knitter and revels in the work of a major project, especially repetitive patterns that become a meditation for his fingers. He has absolutely no problem pulling out many rows of work to fix a mistake he made an hour before. While I would (still) have a crisis at the thought of an hour of work "wasted" or a delay in finishing the project, he's satisfied in calmly repeating the work. Similar to my experiences with exercise, he's found joy in the practice of knitting rather than the achievement of a particular project. That's not to say that he isn't proud of a completed piece, just that he also enjoyed every knit or purl.

Achievement-Orientation Is Learned

Browse the self-help or planner shelves at any Barnes & Noble or the Amazon bestseller list and our obsession with achievement-orientation is clear. There is a huge market for advice on "how to get what you want" and "how to achieve your goals." And while there is certainly a market for advice on mindfulness and living in the present, the books and programs marketed along those lines are quite often *also* about using mindfulness and presence to achieve your goals or boost your productivity. Having picked up this book, I'm sure you're no stranger to these items or marketing messages.

I cracked open a few bestsellers to see exactly how achievement-orientation and overcoming was being sold to us. In the aptly named book *The Achievement Habit,* by Bernard Roth, we learn: "Many reasons are simply excuses to hide the fact that we are not willing to give something a high enough priority in our lives." I've heard this one weaponized and used by life coaches, marketers, and pseudo-spiritual gurus plenty of times to shame people into taking harmful action. Roth goes on to cite an example of a student being late to class because she got a flat tire on her bicycle. Roth claims that if getting to class on time was a high-enough priority, she would have found a way to get there on time. He goes so far as to suggest that if expulsion was the consequence for being late, she'd be early every time.[44] Roth doesn't entertain the idea that her bicycle might be her only mode of transportation, that she doesn't have a friend to call for a ride because they're all at work, or that hitch-hiking isn't safe for a young woman on her own.

We get a similar message in Rachel Hollis's bestseller *Girl, Wash Your Face*. She writes, "When you really want something, you will find a way. When you don't really want something, you'll find an excuse." Getting what you want is your responsibility, which means not getting what you want is your fault.[45] This kind of achievement-orientation assumes a level playing field, equal access to the tools of success. This line of thought led to Hollis unleashing a social media firestorm in 2021 when she posted a video to Instagram where she compared herself to Harriet Tubman and Malala Yousafzai, saying she was proud to be "unrelatable." She claimed that she works hard enough to have a woman who comes to "clean the toilets" twice a week. Hollis doesn't seem to consider that her housekeeper likely works just as hard with far fewer resources. She doesn't consider that her housekeeper's life is likely not full of excuses, but full of structural barriers to upward mobility.[46]

And in Brian Tracy's book *Goals!* we learn that we can erase negative emotions by taking responsibility for every situation we find ourselves in. He exclaims, "Just imagine! You can free yourself from negative emotions and begin taking control of your life by simply saying, 'I am responsible!' whenever you start to feel angry or upset for any reason."[47] I won't deny the power of a mindset shift. But the idea that anger or sadness has no place in life because *we* are responsible for our circumstances is ludicrous. Tracy doesn't entertain the idea that there are circumstances that deserve to be met with anger or that, as Rebecca Traister has powerfully argued in *Good and Mad*, anger can be a galvanizing force for change.[48]

I Can't Get No. . .

Maybe another way to say that we're trained to be achievement-oriented is that we're also trained to be *hungry*. A consumer economy is built on our desire for more. And because "more" is expensive, we're always on the lookout for the next promotion, side gig, or get-rich-quick scheme. Further, research has shown that our happiness (not the same thing as satisfaction, but certainly related) is relative. While we might take pride in an individual achievement, we look to whether we're better off than others in our reference group (e.g., co-workers, family, social group, graduating class) to account for our overall level of happiness.[49] In a 2016 paper for *Social Forces*, Arthur S. Alderson and Tally Katz-Gerro conclude: "Without adjustment by other factors associated with happiness, the more highly people rate their income relative to a reference group or relative to all others that they know, the happier they are, and the relative income effect dominates the absolute income effect." In addition, those who regularly compare their own income achievement to others' report lower happiness overall. Alderson and Katz-Gerro also note that other markers of social status follow a similar pattern to that of income.[50] If you think you take better vacations, live in a nicer house, or drive a more luxurious car than others around you, you will report a higher level of happiness overall. This effect, then, seems to feed our hunger for greater and greater achievement, while it also subverts our agency and values. In other words, driving a more luxurious car might not be something you actually want to do, but if you perceive that car increasing your relative status, you'll believe it will make you happier, too. That happiness, though, is fleeting—a phenomenon that has been called the "hedonic treadmill."

Researchers are always quick to point out that studying happiness is a tough task. Happiness means different things to different people, and there is no quantitative way to measure it. Plus, since our perception of happiness does seem to be relativistic in key ways, evaluating our own overall happiness is a challenge, too. Personally, I'm less interested in evaluating my overall happiness and more interested in cultivating daily satisfaction. The exploration of satisfaction belongs with our exploration of practice and achievement because "being satisfied" is a good way to describe the opportunity that comes from practice, rather than achievement. We use the idea of satisfaction to describe the feeling that comes from sating an appetite—whether for food, sex, learning, or any other hunger. Practice brings on satiety. Sometimes practice feels like the enjoyment of an expensive and artfully prepared meal, and sometimes practice feels like the relief that comes from inhaling a protein bar at the end of a long hike. In my humble opinion, neither is a better experience—they're both extremely satisfying in their own way. Satisfaction is not the end goal, the *telos*, of practice. Rather, it is the state of mind we inhabit when we shift into practice-orientation.

Achievement-orientation—and all of those self-help books about goal-setting and productivity—starts with the assumption that satisfaction is what happens when the goal is achieved or the to-do list is vanquished. But practice-orientation helps us access a state of satisfaction in the pursuit or process. Take writing this book, for instance. Many might assume that the satisfaction is in completing the book. And I'm sure that's true for many people. But I really enjoy writing—it's part of how I process ideas, it allows me to formulate thoughts in a way my autistic brain doesn't like to do in speech. It feels *good* and satisfying to me to write. So writing this book isn't a singular project-based activity. It's part of a larger writing practice that creates a great deal of satisfaction in my life.

Now, that's not to say that everything we do as practice is going to be enjoyable or pleasurable. But I *do* believe that we can find a sense of satisfaction in everything from cleaning to filling out spreadsheets to mowing the lawn. Not just in having done it, but in *doing* it. At the least, there can be satisfaction in the affirmative choice to do a chore or work on a mundane project. Above all, even the tasks that we don't particularly like doing don't need to be a source of misery that only abates when complete. We can find satisfaction in things that are tedious, banal, or obligatory when we make practice our orientation. Writer and activist adrienne maree brown puts it this way in a keynote speech she gave in 2019:

> . . .we must build a felt sense in ourselves of authentic satisfaction. and remember that pleasure is not a frivolous spoil of luxury, but a measure of aliveness, the life force that has been whittled away, stolen away, by oppression and colonization and capitalism. we must break with the assumption of misery that does not serve us.[51]

That last sentence is fascinating to me. At first I read it as, "we must break with the assumption *that* misery does not serve us." But that's not what brown says. She's speaking of an *assumption of* misery, that misery is just part of life, of change, of communities. It echoes what Shani Orgad and Rosalind Gill[52] describe as "normalizing the struggle" that is a core message of the cult of confidence. They point to influencers like Rachel Hollis and former Facebook COO Sheryl Sandberg who further inculcate the story of sacrifice and hard work to achieve success. We assume we have to break our bodies and minds— sometimes our families, too—to get ahead and achieve our goals. At the very least, the merit badges and trophies, the accolades and promotions, give us *some* reward for withstanding the misery, right? Further, the goals we set also work to prevent imagined future misery. We work hard for that promotion because we're afraid of the misery of life lived at our present level of comfort (or discomfort). We lose more weight because we're afraid of the misery of stigma. We push ourselves to recreate the Pinterest-perfect birthday party because we're afraid of the misery of being judged a less-than-stellar parent. We live in a "no pain, no gain" kind of world. Misery is built in, and our fear of it keeps us from realizing that satisfaction is available to us, and so too, brown would argue, is pleasure.

I know that all sounds frighteningly bleak. And you probably don't think about a fear of misery on a regular basis. But again, if you live in the capitalist West, you've been conditioned to hunger for more while denying yourself satisfaction because misery—or pain, or discomfort— must come first. Misery is valorized as a *tool* for achieving satisfaction. It's the subtext written into every page of the self-help palimpsests that crowd the bestseller charts. If you choose the misery that comes with the pursuit of success, you'll be rewarded handsomely. If that were true, though, I think we'd all be a lot happier, more satisfied with our lives. But it seems that misery is only a tool for achieving more misery. Practice, and the satisfaction that comes with it, is a tool for growth and change that operates outside of the achievement-oriented, misery-inducing system. I don't deny that practice can be challenging—and that satisfaction is *not* a given, especially for those in truly difficult circumstances. But I think it's a far better alternative to a gospel of misery.

Reflection:

- What practices have you already established for yourself? How do you experience satisfaction through them?
- Where did you learn your own achievement-orientation? How has it benefitted you? When has it led you astray?
- Do you assume misery (or at least, discomfort) is a prerequisite for satisfaction? Why or why not?

5

Calculating Capacity

I would have liked to say, 'It's okay. I can do this,' but the truth was that
I couldn't.
                                    —Jenny Lawson, *Broken (in the Best Possible Way)*[53]

I CAN'T TELL you how many times I've been asked: Is this goal realistic?
It's a frustratingly difficult question to answer. Whether an objective is
"realistic" depends less on the objective itself and more on the resources
it requires to attain it. Can you build a business that does a million
dollars in revenue in the first year? Absolutely, but you need to invest
capital to build the systems and structure that objective requires. You
likely also need existing connections to workers you can hire, clients
who are ready to deal, and skills to deliver the product or service that
generates the business's revenue. Can you run a marathon this year if
you've never run before? Sure thing, but you'll need plenty of time for
training, a budget for shoes, and decent healthcare to keep your body
functioning.

Of course, having access to resources doesn't guarantee success at
an endeavor. But every "realistic" objective has a minimum set of
resources that it requires to even be possible. Another way to think
of access to resources is capacity. Capacity is the extent of what you

(or a business, family, or organization) can do with the resources you have access to without burning out or breaking down. To know whether an objective is realistic, you have to calculate your capacity.

Capacity is like a budget. When you budget your personal expenses, you calculate how much money you spend on a weekly or monthly basis to sustain your lifestyle, and decide how much money you will allot for discretionary spending and saving. Money is a component of capacity, but capacity has many more facets than your personal budget. Calculating your capacity will include measures for time, physical energy, mental energy, emotional energy, support, and skills. If there are other resources you regularly tap into to support your endeavors, those resources are part of your capacity, too.

The biggest challenge I see people run into with goal-setting isn't whether the goal itself is realistic or whether the goal-setter is sufficiently disciplined. The biggest challenge is that people have no idea what their personal capacity actually is, and so can't take it into account when they're thinking about plans or goals. Positive thinking can't make up for a lack of capacity. We end up failing to meet our objectives because we simply don't have the resources, but often chalk it up to personal failure or lack of willpower. In this chapter, we take a look at some of the components of capacity so that you can better calculate your own or the capacity of any team you manage. I'll tell you

right now that there isn't some delightfully concrete formula for calculating capacity, but by understanding where you might have excess resources and where your resources are strained, you'll have a much better handle on what you can commit to. And that sets the stage for a more satisfying approach to taking on new challenges.

Time

You have the same 24 hours as Beyoncé, the productivity gurus will tell you. And if we're just talking about the measure of time, that's certainly true. But time isn't so much about the time you have to fill and much more how you fill your time. And in this case, Beyoncé has a very, very different 24 hours than you do. According to a 2013 article in the *International Business Times*, Beyoncé and Jay-Z have 88 employees across three properties.[54] While a more recent total of employees doesn't seem to exist, one assumes their team (and property holdings) have grown over the last decade. The exact number doesn't matter so much as the fact that Beyoncé doesn't *only* have 24 hours. She also has the eight-hour workdays of each of her employees. She has people who do her hair and makeup, support her children, and manage her social media. She has people who make travel arrangements for her and coordinate grocery deliveries. In short, Beyoncé uses her time very differently than you and I do. We can't expect to match her output because we don't have the same time resources that she has (nor, I presume, the wealth).

We like to think of time as a concrete, unchanging resource. But time is malleable and relative. It's a resource that is affected by every decision we make—often in ways we're absolutely terrible at measuring. And for good reason! Social theorist Barbara Adam studies the intersection of time and work. She makes the distinction between clock time, an arbitrary quantification of time that allows for exchange (i.e., being paid for the time you work), and time as we actually experience. She writes beautifully about the way we experience time, "time is life; it is change and difference; it is evolution; it is development; it is birth and death, growth and decay; it is the past and future gathered up in the present; it is potential; it is origin and destiny."[55] The reason we struggle to estimate the amount of time a task will take or how long we'll have to work toward a goal is because we do not experience time the way the clock (or calendar) measures it. We know that time moves quickly when we're in a state of flow. When we're waiting for something exciting, time moves slower than molasses. In an emergency, a split second can expand to allow us to process a huge amount of information and make a life or death decision. Plus, some time "costs" us more than others. Certain activities might take all of your concentration or energy, meaning that the rest of your time can't be used for as much.

Maybe your sense of clock time is better than mine. Maybe you have an elaborate system of alarms and reminder notifications to keep you on schedule. Or maybe you live in the moment and try to forget about the clock. However you've managed the duality of clock time and life time, I'm betting you still don't have it down. I certainly don't. There's a good chance you don't account for the time that your various commitments and responsibilities require of you. And it's very likely that you don't measure the time you spend taking care of yourself or your family. This time matters—especially if you don't have personal staff to rely on like Beyoncé does.

Instead of accounting for this time and getting a better handle on the hard limits of our schedules, we buy into notions of productivity and working harder to achieve more. And while there are certainly techniques you can use to make the most of the time you have, the time you have is indeed limited. It's limited by what you've already committed to plus the very real buffers that each commitment has attached to it. By better understanding these limitations, you can more easily assess whether you have the time resources to accept a new responsibility or take on a new project. That's going to require you to say "no" more often than you're likely accustomed to—but it will lead to a more sustainable pace and allocation of resources.

So how do you get a better handle on your time resources? The first tool I'd suggest is a simple time journal. It's like a food journal, if you're familiar with that courtesy of a nutritionist or doctor. Instead of logging what you eat, you log how you spend your time. All of your time. If you're a super Type-A or a dedicated Virgo, you can write down the times of each activity and how long they last. But what's most important are the activities themselves. What exactly are you spending Beyoncé's 24 hours on? Record your journal for at least a week. Honestly, a month is better, but very few people are going to have the time (or patience) to record a time journal for that long.

When I spoke with business operations coach Elisabeth Jackson about making productivity systems more humane, she told me that she has all of her clients keep a time journal. She told me that her clients are pretty surprised when they realize that the answer to the age-old question, "Where did all the time go?" is that it was spent on tasks of little consequence. Elisabeth and I agree that keeping a time journal isn't a matter of trying to squeeze every ounce of productivity out of your time. In fact, Jackson doesn't even like the word *productivity* because it makes her feel like there is a price tag on her time. Instead, the time journal gives you a chance to see whether you're spending your time on things that are important to you or whether that time is being spent on shoulds and supposed-tos.[56]

Likely, as you log your activities, you notice some patterns. You probably don't realize how many times per day you check your email or switch between Slack conversations and the task at hand. You don't realize how long it takes to go grocery shopping or pick up the kids from school. And that's fine—the whole point of the time journal is to better understand how you're already using your time, not to make changes. That said, there's a good chance that logging your time will influence your behavior. Who wants to write down that they checked their email 15 times during their workday? Nobody, that's who. So you start checking your email less simply so that you don't have to write it down. How does that feel? What are the consequences? What are the benefits?

Once you've got your time journal completed, I've found zero-based scheduling very helpful for understanding how my schedule actually works, as opposed to the rose-colored glasses way I think it works. Zero-based scheduling is a technique in which you make every minute of the day an appointment on your calendar. You schedule blocks of time for sleep, coffee, workouts, family time, television, chores, etc. . . . in addition to your work tasks and meetings. When you finish, your schedule is completely filled. The level of detail you use in your zero-based scheduling is up to you. Some people carve out smaller blocks that correspond more to individual tasks, while I carve out larger blocks that give more general guidance (i.e., morning routine, a.m. writing, family time). As with the time journal, the goal with zero-based scheduling isn't to make changes in how you spend your time. It's an observational tool. As you go through your day, especially if you get notifications of your "appointments" to a device you carry with you, you'll notice the limitations of your schedule. You'll notice when you've scheduled two hours, but the task really needs three. You'll notice when there is just too much of a particular kind of activity on one day (ahem, Zoom meetings). And you'll notice when things happen faster than you think they do. As I mentioned earlier, getting clear about your time resources is not the same thing as optimizing for productivity. You might discover inefficiencies or opportunities as you pay closer attention to how you use your time. But that's not the goal of the exercise. The goal, instead, is to make the way you use the time resources you have more intentional.

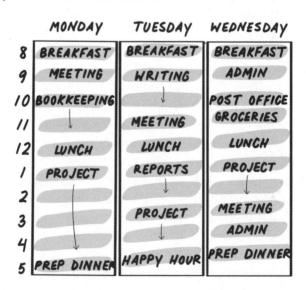

	MONDAY	TUESDAY	WEDNESDAY
8	BREAKFAST	BREAKFAST	BREAKFAST
9	MEETING	WRITING	ADMIN
10	BOOKKEEPING	↓	POST OFFICE
11	↓	MEETING	GROCERIES
12	LUNCH	LUNCH	LUNCH
1	PROJECT	REPORTS	PROJECT
2	↓	↓	↓
3		PROJECT	MEETING
4		↓	ADMIN
5	PREP DINNER	HAPPY HOUR	PREP DINNER

With these two activities completed, consider what you've learned about how you spend your time, what the hard limits on your time are, and how the way you use time impacts your other resources such as physical, mental, or emotional energy. In what ways are you overcommitted? What is taking up time that's unnecessary or unpleasant? What do you wish you had more time for? What are you committed to that you don't often account for in your schedule? I'll get more into time and how we use it later on so, for now, concentrate on observing and learning.

Physical, Mental, and Emotional Energy

"Hey! How are you?"

"I'm tired."

As a society, we live in a state of constant fatigue. Some of it is physical—due to grinding schedules, lack of sleep or rest, or inconsistent eating schedules. Some of it is mental or emotional—due to emotional labor, unrelenting anxiety, or a constant barrage of other people's needs. We've pushed ourselves into a pattern that is unsustainable for the vast majority of bodies and minds. But we just keep at it. Yet, physical, mental, and emotional energies are key to understanding our capacity. Being exhausted means that our physical, mental, and emotional resources are totally tapped out. If you've ever experienced burnout, you know just how impossible it is to accomplish even basic tasks when your physical, mental, and emotional energy is depleted. And you also know how unlikely you are to give yourself a break or adjust your expectations. This only adds to the problem, of course.

And that's why when we talk about capacity, we have to talk about energy. While time, skills, or money deficits may be able to be reallocated to another set of resources, it's really difficult to make up for a lack of energy with other resources. So let's take a look at three ways that your energetic resources are limited: internalized ableism, precarity, and emotional labor.

Internalized Ableism

Ableism, like other oppressive systems, is a belief that what is "natural," "normal," or universally desired is a body that is best suited (or most adapted) to the built world, our modern economic system, accepted communication styles, cultural constructions of beauty or health, or other normalized cultural expectations. It's the bias that makes disability a personal responsibility rather than a recognition that many spaces and social circumstances are exclusionary to people with bodies who do not conform to cultural expectations. Ableism is what prevents us from seeing that a wheelchair is not what makes someone disabled— the lack of a ramp up to a building does. It's what makes stories of overcoming so "inspiring." Ableism is also what makes us label others (or ourselves) lazy or crazy.

In Chapter 2, I detail how the moral systems that we live in create a narrative of overcoming. We're conditioned to see the obstacles in front of us as opportunities for growth instead of the features of exploitative or exclusionary systems. Ableism also contributes to the overcoming narrative. An ableist perspective sees learning to walk— and therefore no longer using a wheelchair—as the desired state. Or, an ableist perspective sees autistic people working to overcome their routines or difficulty with eye contact as virtuous. In an ableist culture, then, we're taught that difference is defect, and the proper course of action is to fix what's broken.

"Fixing" is a major drain on resources. When I'm working against my autistic traits, I'm simply not functioning at my best. But when I'm in an environment that fits my needs, I have many more resources to draw on. One way to think of this drain is with "spoon theory," a system initially created by Christine Miserandino on her blog, *But You Don't Look Sick*. Miserandino wanted to share what it was like to live with lupus with her best friend, who had asked her to describe the experience. Each day, we start with a certain number of spoons. In the case of lupus, every activity is a choice between conserving energy or giving up a spoon. Even simple activities like getting out of bed or making breakfast are a drain on energy reserves.[57] Spoon theory has been widely adopted by disabled, neurodivergent, and even nondisabled people as a way of communicating their capacity to others. As another example, I don't use any spoons going about daily activities like getting out of bed or making breakfast. But interacting with a group of people or even going to the store can cost me a significant number of spoons. I was recently at a family gathering, which I thoroughly enjoyed. I even felt good that evening after I got home. But the next day, I had an anxiety attack at Target merely because I was out of the house longer than I expected to be. And even 48 hours later, I still felt tender and out of sorts. I'd used up a whole weekend's worth of spoons in about four hours.

I think spoon theory has become so widely adopted because it creates a way for us to recognize our own limitations safely. Admitting that the way we operate in the world doesn't quite fit into its sterile, rigid, fast-paced structure feels risky. If we acknowledge our own limitations publicly, then we might not get the promotion or others might treat us differently around the office. Admitting limitations is tantamount to admitting you're not "good enough" to do what you want to do. But physical, mental, and emotional limitations aren't a matter of mindset or positive thinking. There are no personal affirmations or even medication (I'm on several!) that will make my autism go away or prevent me from cycling into depressive episodes. Whatever makes your body different may also present you with limitations.

When ableism is internalized, it means that our ableist bias includes ourselves, our own bodies. We make every accommodation we can to fit into the built world, the modern economic system, or cultural constructions of beauty or health—even if it means constantly denying ourselves pleasure or self-acceptance. In her book *The Body Is Not an Apology*, Sonya Renee Taylor writes, "We must make peace with difference. This is a simple perspective when applied to nature, but oh, how we struggle when transferring the concept onto human forms."[58] Internalized ableism is the violence we do to ourselves as we police our own differences. It's also the violence we do to ourselves when we make it our goal or project to conform to cultural expectations. And it's the violence we do to ourselves when we ignore the physical energy we have (or don't have) to give when we commit to responsibilities or resolutions, winding our way through The Validation Spiral. By including discussion of the harm that internalized ableism does here, I am in no way trying to deny or diminish the violence that is perpetuated through externalized ableism. Nor do I want to diminish the privilege I hold, despite my own limitations, as a thin, white, cis, straight woman.

My autism and anxiety can make it difficult to take care of any task that requires a phone call. I'm easily overstimulated in spaces where there is loud music or many conversations happening at once. I can't make a meal and listen to my child talk to me while there is music playing softly in the room. It's incredibly hard for me to recognize these things as hard limits on my energetic resources, and I think it might be even harder for others to recognize them as hard limits. It's easy for me to call myself lazy (a word that's been banned in our house) or socially awkward. But is it fair to myself or others to assume these negative identities when what I'm really identifying is simply how I'm different? Of course not. And is it really an act of personal growth or self-improvement to set a goal to change these traits in favor of ones that conform to cultural expectations? Of course not—it's an act of personal violence and self-negation.

One way to wrestle with internalized ableism and our 21st-century hustle culture is what Brittany Berger, a marketing consultant and mental health advocate, calls energy management. Like project management or time management, Berger uses energy management as a system for tracking the ebb and flow of her energy as a chronically ill person. In a 2021 interview, she told me: "Energy management is honing your self-awareness around your productivity. Because once you know your energy levels and rhythms and how they fluctuate throughout the day and week, it becomes really easy to know what time of day is best for you to write or what time of day is best for you to do your admin, or take a break. It becomes a lot easier to arrange your life to expend [less] energy [on tasks], but also [expend] energy at the right time."[59] We have as many shoulds and supposed-tos about when to work, eat lunch, sleep, or take a walk as we do about life milestones. For many of us, those shoulds and supposed-tos just don't work. While it's not always possible, it's helpful to structure activities to maximize your energy—regardless of whether that means you're doing something at a "weird" time or not.

When it comes to taking stock of our physical, mental, and emotional energy, internalized ableism makes it difficult to acknowledge our hard limits or depleted reserves. But acknowledging limitations is key to calculating your capacity and choosing a course of action that's equal to the resources you do have access to. It's also key to save yourself from the harm of "pushing through" or "grinding it out." While battling resistance is normal, busting past real limits—which are defined by you, not a manager, client, or the culture—isn't.

Precarity

Now, let's examine precarity. In his 2011 book *The Precariat: A New Dangerous Class*, economist Guy Standing describes an emerging class of workers he dubs—you guessed it—the precariat. He explains that the precariat is made up of people who gig, freelance, temp, or work in other forms of so-called "flexible" structures. They're often highly educated and working below their qualifications. And they lack a defining narrative for their working life. The precariat is also defined by how they're compensated for their work—wages only, no nonwage benefits like paid time off or health insurance. This emerging class is divided into three subgroups: those who have lost the stability of traditional working-class jobs, immigrants and minorities who have limited access to employment to begin with, and educated workers unable to find permanent work commensurate with their qualifications.[60]

I include Standing's conception of the precariat—along with the broader experience of precarity—in discussing capacity because so many systems for planning and goal-setting assume the user works a salaried desk job five days a week, with paid time off and fully funded healthcare, and that the greatest challenge to stability is having to navigate carpool for the soccer team. Perhaps professionals who read about time management or achieving goals 20 years ago predominantly fell into that category. But today, the reality is very, very different. When I worked at a Borders Books and Music in the early 2000s, there were a number of full-time employees who had graduate degrees. Almost all of us had undergraduate degrees. We used to joke that we were the overeducated and underpaid club (my salary as a manager working 50 to 60 hours per week was $28,000 per year). There is no guarantee of finding "good work" today no matter your qualifications or connections—and there hasn't been for some time.

In fact, I'm more likely to assume that you're a member of the precariat than you are a member of the salariat, as Standing calls it.

And that means you have a lot on your plate. Your ability to pay your bills might depend on whether your hunt for the next freelance gig is successful. Your need to access basic medical care might mean you dip into your savings account, if you even have one. And a vacation? Well, that sounds nice. Even if you do find yourself with a full-time, permanent, salaried job or you're a business owner with steady revenue, your capacity is still influenced by the structural shifts that have led to the explosion of the precariat—401(K)s instead of pensions, health savings accounts instead of fully-funded insurance, and don't forget mounds of student debt. Navigating all of this takes a lot of spoons.

Plus, precarity, broadly speaking, can take many forms beyond financial precarity: health precarity, interpersonal precarity, home and housing precarity, and other forms of uncertainty and instability. Precarity isn't a personal failing—although it's often perceived as such. It's the outcome of the systems we live in. Precarity is both a result of neoliberal meritocratic policy and its enforcing condition. We're precarious because of neoliberal policies, and precarity is what keeps us working for the system.

Anne Helen Petersen explores our shared states of precarity in her book *Can't Even*. While the book is focused on the Millennial experience, Petersen is quick to point out that the conditions that have created such ubiquitous burnout among that group are endemic to all generations in the United States. We like to believe that the conditions we are subject to don't necessarily create a drain on our resources. We like to believe this because consumer culture conditions us to believe this. The less we can tie our problems to systems and circumstances outside our control, the more likely we are to buy the solutions companies sell us. The rise of self-care capitalism, fitness wearables and sleep trackers, and meal delivery services are all illustrative of this. We end up using *other* resources (time and money, most often) to shore up the physical, mental, and emotional energy that precarity impinges on. Petersen describes the impact of precarity like this, "The only way to make it all work is to employ relentless focus—to never, ever stop moving."[61] How could precarity be anything other than a drain on our energetic resources? Now, calculating the exact measure of that drain isn't really possible. But acknowledging it—especially when you're dealing with a situational setback or a failure of the system—can help make sense of your exhaustion. That can be enough to help you rethink your commitments and responsibilities so that you can build more satisfaction back into your life.

Emotional Labor

Finally, let's talk about emotional labor. *Emotional labor* is a term coined by sociologist Arlie Russell Hochschild in her 1983 book *The Managed Heart*. Hochschild did an exhaustive study of flight attendants to take a look at an extreme example of the performance of emotional labor. Flight attendants must make customers feel safe and welcome, manage unruly passengers, and provide a sense of stability in what is an anxiety-inducing experience for many people. The emotional work flight attendants do is perhaps their core responsibility, despite the pilot reminding us that they're there primarily for our safety. What Hochschild observed as she developed her theories on emotional labor is that, "Beneath the difference between physical and emotional labor there lies a similarity in the possible cost of doing the work: the worker can become estranged or alienated from an aspect of self—either the body or the margins of the soul—that is used to do the work."[62]

Maybe you think it's easy to put on a smile or speak calmly and confidently when a passenger has a fit about checking the bag that doesn't fit in the overhead compartment. But, when it's in the job description, it takes on a different quality and requires precious energetic resources. Even if we're not flight attendants (and if you are, thanks for being awesome), we do emotional work every day. It comes with the territory of being a human who interacts with other humans. When you purposefully hold back your frustration the third time your kid asks for water at bedtime, that's emotional work. When you negotiate what's for dinner with your partner, that's emotional work. It's regulation and management of the outward display of our inner emotional signals. *Emotional labor*, as Hochschild defines it, is when that emotional work becomes part of a value exchange—in other words, when you're getting paid to smile or keep your cool.

As the service sector and knowledge work has taken over the economy, almost all of us have forms of emotional labor in our job descriptions. For you, it might happen directly with customers or clients. Or, you might perform emotional labor in managing a team or recruiting partners. Maybe your emotional labor is less about putting on a smile and more about retaining a calm demeanor in fraught circumstances. However you end up performing emotional labor, it impacts your ability to identify your true feelings and emotional states outside of work. As Hochschild describes it, you start to become "estranged or alienated" from what's really true for you. You start to identify with the performance of an emotional state rather than what you're actually feeling. While that might be helpful in the short term, it's a real burden on resources over the long term.

In Chapter 3, which discusses identity, I describe how the platforms we rely on for work—whether that's creator platforms like YouTube, gig platforms like Uber, or the platform that is the company you work for—can estrange us from our own sense of identity. Emotional labor is one of the mechanisms at work. Over the last few years, I started to notice how much emotional labor I was doing every time I posted to Instagram, which is a platform I use for work rather than pleasure. The times I find it most difficult to come up with something to post are the times when my emotional energy reserves are at their lowest. It became clear to me that, in order to use the platform, I needed to account for the emotional resources it required in the rest of my workload. Yes, posting takes time but it takes *more* emotional labor, at least for me.

That brings me to another aspect of emotional labor—and one that draws on our previous explorations of internalized ableism and precarity as influences on our physical, mental, and emotional energy. And that aspect is how all sorts of differences and forms of precarity can make the performance of emotional labor all the more draining. For me, my autism limits my capacity to perform emotional labor—not so much because I'm bad at it but because I'm *constantly* doing active emotional work when others might be able to relax and passively rely on social intuition. As I look over my history of burnout and depression, I can link each cycle to overextending myself on account of emotional labor. If I don't regularly check in with my capacity for emotional work,

I'm likely to drain myself dry. Honestly, this has probably been the most profound realization since my diagnosis.

You may not be autistic—but maybe you're diagnosed with ADHD or generalized anxiety. Your experience will be different than mine but the result is the same: there is an unaccounted for drain on your energetic resources. Maybe, just maybe, you don't have any such diagnosis. But you're going through a divorce, you just had a kid, you're switching careers, or you're moving into a new house. These are also *huge* drains on your energetic resources. We know those things are exhausting physically and mentally, but I think we often ignore the impact on our emotional energy. Each situation that influences your emotional energy needs to be accounted for when you try to take stock of your capacity. Otherwise, internalized ableism will likely tell you to suck it up, think positively, and "soldier on."

Money and Skills

To this point, I've looked at what drains our resources and limits our capacity. Certainly money and skills can be drained or felt as limitations. But, they're also incredibly powerful resources that have the ability to cover a lot of ground for other resources—and that's what I'm going to focus on here.

First, I want to acknowledge that each reader comes to this book with a different net worth. Each reader also comes with a different set of priorities for how they spend their money. And so every reader is going to take something different away from this section. But whether you're living paycheck to paycheck, living beyond your means, or feeling rather comfortable, I encourage you to come to this topic with an open mind. Don't worry, I won't ask you to manifest more money, put expenses on a credit card to prove you're "invested," or just think positively about money. Instead, I want to encourage you to look at money as a tool you can use to get stuff done.

When we use money as a tool to ease the depletion of other resources, it can be a game-changer. That doesn't mean you have to spend money you don't have. Small expenditures can help you reclaim much more valuable capacity. I'll give you a personal example. Last spring, I started to get groceries delivered. The grocery store my husband and I prefer is about 15 minutes away and often involves sitting in traffic. Not only is that a drain on time, but it's a drain on my mood. At first, grocery delivery was free—I just had to pay the tip for the driver. That was a no-brainer. Spending an extra $10 or $12 was well worth the time I got back as well as the opportunity to do a mood-boosting activity like taking a walk. But this winter, our grocery store added a $10 delivery charge on top of the tip we pay the driver. Now, getting groceries delivered was a $20 or more prospect. It would be easy to say, "No way am I paying $20 for the convenience of getting groceries delivered!" And I absolutely had that reaction at first. But then I started to think about the how much that hour was worth to me—not in terms of what I get paid but in terms of what I'm willing to spend. Instead of thinking about paying extra for groceries, I thought about whether I was willing to spend $20 to take a long walk and listen to a podcast. While you might not make the same decision, my answer was that, yes, it *is* worth it. Not every time. But when I both need groceries *and* I need some time to myself to recharge, it's worth it. We can also think of our friend Beyoncé here. Beyoncé buys other people's time by hiring them. She uses money as a resource to vastly increase the number of hours she has available—both her own and other people's.

Money can buy therapy, a gym membership, or a massage to boost our physical, mental, or emotional energy. It can ease our cognitive burden by buying us software that is easier to use. Money can buy us education or training. It can buy us consulting or coaching. I don't mean to be flippant about money here, but I *do* mean to not be precious about it. Thanks to the precarity of our economic system and the consumer culture we live in, money is often put in a venerated category of its own. However, I've found that grouping money in with all of the other resources gives me a better perspective on how I can pad the accounts of those resources that are more scarce to me than money.

Skills can operate similarly. While it takes time (and sometimes money) to learn a new skill, a new skill can help you save time, protect your energy, and even make you more money. Think of all the things you've learned how to do to avoid paying someone else, too. You probably learned to cook to avoid paying for takeout every night. Maybe you learned how to use Photoshop so you didn't need to pay a photographer or an editor to fix your family portraits. Or you learned how to operate QuickBooks so you didn't have to pay a bookkeeper. While I'm not a DIY-at-all-costs advocate—far from it—I do appreciate the value of learning a skill to save on other resources.

Renewable Resources

There's one more facet of calculating your capacity that I want to cover here and that's how you renew your resources and replenish your capacity. You know the common advice: meditate, sleep more, eat well, get a hobby, turn off your phone. I'm not going to repeat that. It's quite dull. Fine, most of those things work. But we end up moralizing them and making ourselves feel bad when we don't (or can't) do them— which isn't great for our capacity. I'm way more concerned with what activities (or nonactivities) renew *you*. What ways of using your time help you feel satisfied and fulfilled? What activities reenergize you? What helps you most when you feel your emotional resources are exhausted? What recharges your creativity?

In Chapter 4, I introduce the idea of interdependence and systems thinking. Calculating your capacity is an exercise in extreme systems thinking. Not only does it require us to identify shoulds and supposed-tos that don't serve us and drain our capacity, it also requires us to see the give and take between different limitations, commitments, and resources. If you find yourself in the midst of financial precarity, you might need to lean on your skills more. If you find yourself with a hard limit on your time due to your health, you might need to lean more on money. But even if your overall capacity is very low (now or always), having a clear picture of that will help you make the best decisions for you. You'll be able to more intentionally allocate your resources, giving each a distinct purpose—a practice that can greatly increase your satisfaction without trying to make big changes.

Exercise:

Conduct a capacity audit. Use the following prompts to take stock of your resources in each area. This can also be a helpful activity to do with your partner, family, or team at work.

Time

- What's already on your calendar?
- What routines or recurring tasks do you need to make space for?
- What life priorities do you often skip over because of time?
- How much time do you really have to devote to new projects?

Energy

- When is your energy up? When is your energy down?
- What responsibilities or projects take up more energy than others? Why?
- What activities help you feel more energized? Why?
- What tasks do you find mentally draining right now? Why?
- What tasks make you feel on top of things? Why?
- When is your mental processing power at its best? When is it less reliable? Why?

Health

- How is your mental and emotional health impacting your capacity?
- Do you have the space to feel your feelings?
- Have you committed to habits or activities that support your overall wellness?
- How is your physical health impacting your capacity?

Money

- What money is available to you to invest?
- Do you have any financial leaks that need to be plugged up?
- How could spending more on an aspect of your life or business help you create additional resources?
- How could spending less create more ease?

Support and Community

- Who can you rely on for support?
- What would you like to do that could be done by someone else?

- What shared resources can you draw on for support?
- Who needs your support and for what?

Skills and Knowledge

- What skills can you leverage?
- How does your knowledge or expertise give you an advantage?
- How could your past experiences be a liability to you?

6

Growth without Striving

One of the most important discoveries I made in the process of being ill is that solitary striving, my American habit of self-focus, was in some fundamental way a degradation of the most powerful aspects of our lives, which now seem to me to be our interconnectedness and need of others.
—Meghan O'Rourke, *The Invisible Kingdom: Reimagining Chronic Illness*[63]

A FEW YEARS ago, I sat with a small group of business owners in a cute condo in Whitefish, Montana. I was there to facilitate a retreat where each business owner had time to share a current project, challenge, or opportunity, and workshop it with the group. These business owners were all quite successful in their own ways as well as being thoughtful and compassionate. They valued hearing others' experiences and answering their colleagues' fresh questions. Each took their own turn over the time we had together. As the retreat neared its end, only a couple of business owners were left to share with the group. Finally, one of them, Rita Barry, spoke up. Barry's advertising agency had seen explosive growth over the previous two years, so I was curious what she was going to bring to the table.

She said, "The question I've been trying to answer for myself is: What does growth without striving look like?" The whole group, myself included, sat in stunned silence for a minute. What does growth without striving look like? That question seared itself into my brain. Barry and I share a similar personality type and experience as overachievers. We both like awards, trophies, and merit badges. In fact, Barry still has her laminated straight-A report cards from school. We've always excelled, and we've always felt the pressure to excel even more. As if our excellence could prove we were good and worthy enough to take up our little patch of earth and air.

Recently, Barry told me that, while her accomplishment might have looked fairly effortless on the outside, on the inside, she was a bundle of stress and anxiety. She lost clumps of hair as a teenager when the stress started to manifest physically. Because she grew up with financial need, Barry knew her future depended on her ability to wow colleges with her smarts and potential for success. She said, "Everything was about achievement and external validation, even though I didn't actually think of it that way. . . . It never occurred to me that there was an option that wasn't that. To me, that was striving. That's just how I lived and how I felt all that."[64]

I don't think that *striving* is necessarily a negative word. But it's an apt way to describe the anxiety-ridden push toward a goal. It's not only battling resistance or rising to the challenge—but doing so with an acute fear of major consequences if you don't. Not all of us experience the level of striving that Barry describes, but I think we've all had a sense of it. Similarly, not all of us approach goal-setting in a striving manner, but we've probably all had the experience of feeling like "everything is riding on this." Striving is a natural byproduct of the many cultural systems we've talked about to this point. We strive because we're told it's our personal responsibility to succeed (or at least survive) despite the brokenness of everything around us. We strive because our economic salvation depends on it. We strive because we experience precarity and internalized ableism. We strive to prove that we're valuable members of society. We strive because we believe attaining more than our family or friends will make us happier. And we strive to live up to the questionable stories that self-help influencers turn into advice for good living. Rachel Hollis, writing of discouraging experiences, offers up this advice to strivers: "Rend your garments and wail to the heavens like some biblical mourner. Get it all out. Then dry your eyes and wash your face and keep on going. You think this is hard? That's because it is. So what? Nobody said it would be easy."[65] This is the affect of striving. In other words, if it feels like everything is riding on your ability to achieve that next goal, there's a damn good reason.

So what does growth without striving look like? Thanks to Barry, I've made this a central question of my work over the last few years—as well as the central question of this book. Now that I've unpacked what I argue creates the condition for such self-destructive striving, I want to explore our alternatives. To do that, I begin with common feelings that arise during the process of this deconstruction: disorientation and alienation, and how we might get reoriented and reconnected to our sense of purpose.

I'm Not Lost, I'm Exploring. . .

It's entirely possible to feel disoriented and alienated from yourself before you start to recognize the systems that have inspired your goal-setting and, likely, some negative self-talk. So many of the systems we operate in are designed to make us feel that way. Disoriented people are more likely to keep working harder and harder, buying more and more. But once you do start to acknowledge those systems and examine how they've impacted your life, there's a good chance that your response will be, "Well, now what?!" It's certainly what my response was—along with many other people I've talked with. What do I do now if washing my face and getting back to the grind isn't actually serving me?

To be disoriented is to be directionless. What do I actually want? Where do I hope to end up? What am I working toward? The answers to these questions are often supplied by culture; one thing the neoliberal meritocracy myth and the advice industry that props it up give us is a sense of direction. All that emphasis on personal responsibility and proving oneself valuable to society might not be a particularly healthy direction, but it's a direction nonetheless. It's the stuff New Year's resolutions, self-help journals, and productivity apps are made of. When we deconstruct all of the conditioning that gave us direction and orientation in the past, we have to reconstruct a new way to orient ourselves. Some of it might look very similar from the outside—but the motivation behind it will be drastically different.

When your direction has been your identity and that direction is not your own, the result is self-alienation. Our desire feels foreign. Our values seem exotic. We don't know who we are without the systems that have, up until now, formed a major part of our identities. Who am I (and why am I valuable) if not a "productive worker," or "goal-oriented business owner," or "next in line for a promotion?" Earlier, I looked at the question: Who am I without the doing? For many of us, a sense of alienation—otherness—is what's left when we contemplate the essence of our selves without the doing we identify with. Strip away the shoulds and supposed-tos and it can be difficult to know who you are underneath.

We end up disoriented and alienated because the systems we operate in teach us who we are and what we care about—even when our sense of self and personal values are at odds with that conditioning. C. Thi Nguyen's philosophy of games provides a framework for analyzing this phenomenon. Nguyen explains that game designers tell us what to care about by creating a points system and defining the conditions for winning the game. Games—whether they're sports, board games, video games, or party games—necessarily simplify values and goals, providing the structure for play. In playing a game, we temporarily take on those values and goals for the pleasure of the experience.[66]

If we view systems like neoliberalism or supremacy culture through this lens, we can imagine the rules, goals, and point system that we use to play the game. They might very well be things that we take for granted as desirable or morally good: get married, go to college, land a job, purchase a home, have children, and so on. But why are these things so desirable (if not to you individually then certainly within our culture)? Are they things you care about or have you been taught to care about these things? I'm not suggesting, of course, that any of those things are *bad*. I've done them all. But I did them less because I really, really wanted to and more because our systems are designed to make life easier if I do them. Getting married and buying a house—there are tax breaks associated with each of those. Landing a good job means health insurance and paid time off. Going to college creates the potential for a solid middle-class life. The incentives are clear. The points system is well-defined.

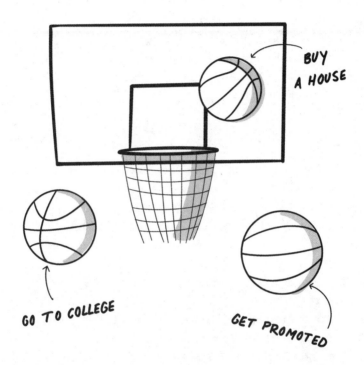

BUY A HOUSE

GO TO COLLEGE

GET PROMOTED

But unlike in a game, the values and end goals of our economic and cultural systems aren't something we take up voluntarily or temporarily. The constraints of the systems we inhabit are enduring and compulsory. Sure, you can play around and break all the rules but, at some point, the system is going to make that really hard for you. Nguyen writes, "Games offer us a momentary experience of value clarity. They are a balm for the existential pains of real life." These systems do offer value clarity—but at the expense of a more nuanced experience of the world. They reduce the discomfort of self-authorship but increase our sense of alienation or disorientation any time we pause to reflect on our lives. Here, what works is balance. We must (re)discover our own desires and purpose and use them to navigate existing systems while—I hope—trying to change those systems. We must recognize the points systems that provide structure to our lives and create new structures that allow for a more nuanced and humane perspective. Structure, whether explicit and overt or implicit and loosely held, is a key part of how we function. You don't have to identify as particularly organized or systems-oriented to recognize structure as an important part of your life. Structure can be as simple as the set of values your action and decision-making is based on. Or, it can grow to include things like habits and routines. Your structure likely needs some sort of purpose to feel like it matters.

Goals versus Commitments

Goals are the basic building blocks of achievement-oriented structure. And while it doesn't have to be the case, that means how we strive to achieve those goals becomes part of the foundation of our life structure. Commitments, on the other hand, are the basic building blocks of practice-oriented structure. Commitments give direction to personal values, create a presence of mind, and help you connect to the evolution of your core identity. Commitments help you reorient without reintroducing striving.

Let's look at an example. Your goal might be to lead a major project at work this year. That's pretty solid. Leading a project would give you exposure to the higher-ups who will think of you the next time a promotion comes up. It'll also give you a chance to explore a strategic or creative element of your work. Plus, leading a project will help you forge new relationships with colleagues. For you, a goal like this may or may not involve striving. It may or may not be something you believe you're supposed to do rather than something you really want to do. It's not a bad goal (and it's not that goals are bad). But the structure and impact of this goal are limited. This goal isn't doing much to provide direction or reconnection outside of the office. It's probably pretty estranged from the things that make up your identity, and likely, it doesn't help you fulfill your personal values, either.

A commitment might be: Raise your hand. "Raise your hand" has a broad scope. It conjures memories of when you had an answer to a question, volunteered yourself, and voted for your preference. It affirms your agency and applies at work as well at home and in your relationships.

At work, raising your hand might simply be a practice of being seen or heard from more often. It might mean you volunteer for more responsibility. And yes, it might mean you lead a major project. At home, raising your hand might be tackling that project you've been meaning to do for ages. It might be offering your partner or child additional support. And it might mean (I hope it does) acknowledging your own needs more often. "Raise your hand" is a commitment to practice values like reliability, creativity, leadership, or spontaneity.

When you make a commitment first, you don't throw out more concrete objectives or projects. It means those objectives and projects are grounded in purpose and in service of your commitment. A commitment provides orientation and direction across a broad range of challenges, decisions, opportunities, and daily tasks. And commitments remind you of your values and vision every time you practice them; they're identity-affirming. Commitments move us toward the self-transforming mind that Robert Kegan describes. They give us a way to take a step back from reflexive action by making our personal frameworks self-evident. When we externalize our values and desires in that way, we're better able to take in new information that might lead to fresh analysis of something we thought we knew or wanted. Plus, commitments give us opportunities to make meaning every day. While a goal might be excellent structure for achieving a specific outcome, a commitment is excellent structure for ensuring the things we do actually mean something to us.

Personal Values

In Chapter 7, you can create a personal vision you can use to orient your commitments, and later, your projects and plans. But before you do, let's talk about personal values. Now, I'm going to guess that if you've picked up this book, there's a good chance that some other productivity, leadership, or self-improvement writer has asked you to name your personal values and given you a big list of values to choose from. On the odd chance you have no idea what I'm talking about, I offer a common way to identify the ideas and characteristics you really value. But I also want to speak to the philosophical and psychological aspects of identifying personal values (because I love some context).

Personal values are how you define what is most important, meaningful, and beneficial to you. They're big picture objectives that help you define what is good and what is bad according to your own personal ethic. We likely borrow personal values from the traditions, culture, and family we grew up in, especially early in life. But as we develop into the self-authoring phase and on into the self-transforming phase, we edit or refine those values.

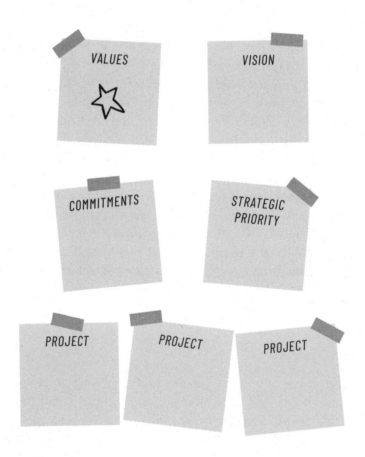

Clearly defining your personal values can seem like busywork—especially if you've done it before. But it's an essential task when we've existed for so long in systems that tell us what to care about, often in opposition to our true values. Again, if we consider Nguyen's philosophy of games, we can see the homogenizing effect that these systems have on our values. We come to see success, independence, and prosperity as values we can all agree on—instead of as values that we've been taught to care about. Cultures and communities will naturally form around shared values—but those shared values should be in harmony with our own personal values and beliefs. And when systems create value structures that oppose our own value structures, we should be able to identify that clearly so that we can make intentional decisions and take appropriate action. So, yeah, we need to pause to reconsider our values in light of the deconstruction we've done to this point.

There are many visualizations and exercises you can do to help you identify your values. Most are free and just a search engine away. But a quick search will also return a long list of personal values that have been aggregated over time from things people say they value. My preference? Take a look at one of those massive lists—or even several—and write down every value that feels important and meaningful *to you*. For instance, you might recognize that "honesty" is important. But does it have a special importance or meaning for you? If not, that's okay. It doesn't mean you're cool with dishonesty. It just means that it's not a driving force in your life. On the other hand, maybe "transparency"—a variation on honesty—*does* have special meaning and importance to you. Transparency, then, might be one of your personal values.

Once you've short-listed maybe 10–20 values, look for patterns. Which are similar? Where is there overlap? What word better describes a grouping you've made from the shortlist? Ideally, you're going to get this list down to about three to five. These are the concepts that you want to guide you, the concepts you hope others see in you. Once you have the winners, jot down a few behaviors that demonstrate each of these values. What do you do that signals that you hold these values? For instance, if transparency is one of your values, you might write down that you avoid saying "fine" when a friend of family asks how you are, and instead, give a specific answer. Or, you might say that you have weekly money meetings with your partner so that you both know what's going on with the finances. This is called "operationalizing your values," and it helps to make your values feel real and integrated.

Now, you should have a working list of personal values, as well as a few behaviors for each that help you recognize how these values are integrated into your daily life. This list is not set in stone—you'll refine it over the course of your life. But it gives you something to work with from this point on.

The psychologist and researcher Edwin Locke pioneered goal-setting theory. A *goal*, as Locke uses the word, is the intended result of any action—not necessarily a particular achievement. Or, as Locke defines it, "ideas of the future, desired end states." So we're talking lower-case-g goals, as opposed to capital-G Goals. Locke's theory deals with goals as the origin of action (i.e., I don't want to be hungry anymore, so I'll eat lunch). But Locke also gestures toward higher-level questions that can be explored in relation to goal-setting theory, the first being: *Where do goals come from?* Here, he points to motives and values—what's driving us and what's important to us. The second higher-level question Locke poses is: *Where do the motives and values come from?*[67] You might guess that this is the question that excites me the most—and why the entire first half of this book is devoted to exploring the origin of many of the beliefs and motivations that have become "common sense" in our productivity-obsessed culture.

Here, Locke posits that motives and values come from needs, but also acknowledges that this doesn't explain the varied motives and values we experience as humans who all share basic needs. I'm not a psychologist, and so I'm not going to suggest an alternative theory to apply with broad strokes. However, I do think that this is an important question for personal inquiry, especially in light of the deconstruction we've already done. Where do *your* personal values come from? What motivates you, and why? Is there a particular need, narrative, or system that's influencing your motives or values? The answers to these questions can be neutral—no need to assign moral value to any answer. But you can ask yourself whether the sources of your personal values and motives are things that you want to influence you on the most fundamental level.

This is the perfect time to bring Rita Barry, the advertising agency owner who was on the retreat in Montana, back into the picture. Barry likes to work hard. She likes to make big things happen. She likes to pursue her edges and improve her skills. She just didn't want to strive—and she didn't want to feel like everything was riding on her striving. She told me, "I can still work really hard and want to achieve, but it's no longer about what that means about me. Am I worthy if I'm a failure? If I do [fail], it's just neutral." What this tells me is that Barry didn't just examine her goals or even her personal values; she examined where her motivation and values were derived from. Some of it she threw out—anything that made her believe it was a personal failing if a project didn't turn out the way she hoped—and some of it she kept. She rebuilt the source of her motivation and values in a way that affirmed her worthiness and set about new projects based on that.

We exist in a multiplicity of systems designed to make us question our worthiness and personal values. Those same systems insist on making meaning for us and supplying us with proper motivation. So any time we try to answer the question, "What does growth without striving look like?" it's imperative that we examine what growth means to us and how the goals that we might be most likely to strive toward are motivated by the system rather than genuine desire. Nguyen offers a way to think about this, too. He describes what happens when our own thick, nuanced values are superseded by simplistic metrics—a process he calls value capture. Value capture occurs when we start to prioritize earning points in a flattened value system rather than creating room to examine rich and subtle forms of value in our lives. Nguyen offers the example of setting a goal to "get fit" and then becoming obsessed with the metrics on your FitBit or watch.[68] Fitness tracker metrics do *not* tell you how fit you are. They can certainly be useful and fun—but they can just as easily inspire obsessive behavior. The same thing can easily happen in our lives with less explicit points systems. Earlier, I mentioned things like buying a home or getting married. If you imagine those milestones as associated with "experience points" and then the ways that points continue to accrue as you keep paying your mortgage or avoid getting divorced, you can see how easy it is gamify the tax code or social structures while missing out on the complex experience of making a home or growing into a relationship.

When I interviewed coach and writer Mara Glatzel about how her personal values play out in her business, she told me that she had to decide whether she was ambitious because she was ambitious, or whether she was ambitious because of capitalism. After some intro-spection, she came to the conclusion that her ambition was indeed intrinsic. But questioning the motivation behind her ambition gave her new parameters for how to support herself. She told me, "In order to produce the way I like to, I need to make a tandem commitment to my own energetic capacity."[69] Glatzel recognizes that her productivity is linked to her capacity—not an act of neglecting her own body or mind in the name of ambitious goals. If growth *with* striving is more familiar to you than growth *without* striving, you might consider making a similar commitment. What are the necessary conditions for more easeful growth or humane ambition for you? Can you meet those conditions on your own or with support? And if not, how can your expectations for growth shift so that you have what you need to move forward without jeopardizing your well-being?

Self-Efficacy

Earlier, I referenced Edwin Locke's goal-setting theory. His work builds on behavioral and motivational theories developed by Albert Bandura. One of Bandura's core concepts is self-efficacy. Self-efficacy is the confidence we have in our ability to take the necessary actions to produce our desired results. To act with self-efficacy signifies a sense of agency and relative power within our environment.[70] If you lack self-efficacy (no shame in that), you might often feel like a ship at the mercy of waves of uncertainty. Self-efficacy as a concept is important within our larger consideration of goals, growth, and striving because we need to both understand the environment we exist in (including political, social, and economic systems) while *also* nurturing a sense of agency. This is the "both/and" that Barry and Glatzel described.

I also heard the hallmarks of self-efficacy in my conversation with Sarah Avenir back in 2020. Avenir is a writer, designer, strategist, and, at the time, the CEO of &yet, a digital strategy agency. She is an all-around renaissance woman. I set up the interview to ask her about how she was leading her team through uncertainty given the pandemic. She told me that "after the initial shake of the snow globe," she realized she had two choices. "One [choice] is to freeze up and try to hold on to everything that you have, try to figure it out and strategize how to keep your things safe. And then the other [choice] is to say, 'well, I never really had much control over this anyway. I guess I might as well just be who I am and allow this to help me take more risks.'" Avenir easily recognized that the environment she was operating in was changing every day, that her employees were scared, and that her clients might be wary of taking on new projects. She used that uncertainty to her advantage, launching creative projects to showcase the agency's unique philosophy on digital development and community building.[71]

You can recognize the influence of systems like neoliberal meritocracy, capitalism, and ableism, while also affirming your own intrinsic desire for growth and ability to act on your own behalf. In fact, recognition of this "both/and" is essential. Acknowledging the duality is the only way to analyze what motivates a particular goal or desire. Growth, of course, doesn't have to look like ambition or massive results. Self-efficacy exists whether your goal is to get a big promotion, double your revenue, or take copious amounts of vacation every year and rest. Bottom line: There are things we can do to create a satisfying life. And if it feels like satisfaction is outside your grasp, it's worth questioning whether what you believe will satisfy you is just what external systems say happiness is made from. To be clear, I'm not suggesting that we're all going to live in mansions, drive fancy cars, and wear luxurious clothes, nor do I discount the profound pain of poverty or loss. But I do believe that it's possible to take self-efficacious action to embody satisfaction. This action and its fruits are the root of self-esteem and worthiness. We affirm ourselves, our needs, and our desires every time we take action that we believe will impact life for the better. From here, we need to define what impacting life for the better looks like for ourselves. In other words, what is the life you want to create for yourself? Then, from there, you can create a structure for practicing self-efficacy by setting commitments.

Exercise:

Use a search engine to find a list of personal values. Make a list of 10–20 values that have special meaning for you. From there, group values that have similar qualities and consider whether there is a word that better describes that meaning of that group to you. Keep honing your list until you have 3–5 core personal values.

For each of those core personal values, list at least five actions that are examples of those values in daily life.

Example:

Curiosity

- *Approach potential conflicts with questions instead of accusations*
- *Learn something new every day*
- *Ask "why" before trying to solve a problem*
- *Gather information from diverse sources before coming to a conclusion*
- *Fill news feeds with challenging ideas*

How do your personal values relate to the values of the systems or institutions you interact with? Are they compatible or mutually exclusive? How will leaning into your true personal values impact your position in the wider world?

7

Choosing Your Destination

Understanding the why behind what you're making allows you to
uncover your intent and potential.
— Abby Covert, *How to Make Sense of Any Mess*[72]

WHO DO YOU want to become? It's time to return to this question. In Chapter 3, I take a close look at identity and explore the concept of the network self. We can think about who we are as a web of interconnected identities based on our psychology, biology, and relationships. Because that web of identities changes over time, our sense of self evolves, too. When we make deliberate choices about the identities we take on and the ones we let go of, we become agents of our own growth. When we decide to take on a new identity, it doesn't diminish our other identities. When we decide to let go of an identity, we can still acknowledge the role of that identity in our lives. New identities are the natural result of curiosity or new discoveries. Similarly, to let go of an identity doesn't mean failure—some identities serve us for a period of time before fading into the background.

As I've mentioned before, I started to make some profound personal changes about five years ago. But it wasn't until a key experience catalyzed a whole new vision of who I wanted to become that I realized just how profoundly my identity would shift. I had just finished leading a small retreat in Montana, and my husband and mother-in-law had planned a special activity for the morning after. They told me what we were doing, but I had no real point of reference for it. Luckily, I had all the nervous energy from the retreat still, so I just went with the plan. After breakfast, we drove up Big Mountain, overlooking the Flathead Valley. Near the top of the mountain, there's a ski resort. This was June, so even though there were still patches of snow at this elevation, we weren't going skiing. Instead, we were going to ride a ski lift up to the very top of the mountain and then hike down to our starting point.

At 34 years old, I hadn't been on many hikes. But I knew that I didn't like walking uphill, let alone hiking up a mountain. So this sounded like the perfect way to enjoy a day in nature. The ski lift ride was a first for me. Growing up pretty poor, I never went skiing (still haven't, but it's on my shortlist). So that was eye-opening in and of itself. At the top of the mountain, there was a viewpoint where you could look out over the Rocky Mountains into Glacier National Park and Waterton Lakes National Park in Canada. For a girl from the mid-Atlantic, it was an unbelievable sight. After a quick bathroom break (I never miss the chance to take advantage of indoor plumbing), we headed out. My mother-in-law Pam was jazzed to be sharing this experience with me and, had I not already been excited, her energy would have infected me in short order.

We started down the Danny On Trail, first through the tiny pine trees and brush just around the tree line, then on into the bigger ponderosa pines and tamaracks. The sides of the trail were dotted colorfully with spring wildflowers—purple, pink, and blue. Pam identified each flower as we walked by, sometimes stopping to look for early huckleberries. The air was crisp but the sun was warm. I felt my chest expand as my heart swelled with pure joy (and much cleaner air than my lungs were used to). I was *in love*. I loved the soft trail under my feet, the tall trees flanking the path, the view of immense Flathead Lake, the air on my skin, and the feeling that I was doing exactly what I wanted to be doing in that moment.

People talk about "mountaintop experiences" as those situations in which their positive emotions, along with intoxicating happy hormones, almost overwhelm their system. They end up high on the vibe of whatever they're doing and who they're with. I'd had plenty of mountaintop experiences before being on this particular mountaintop—but I felt the profundity of this experience in a new way. It wasn't just fun; it was transformative. I was a different person when I came off that mountain, and I had a new vision for who I wanted to become. I'm approaching my 40th birthday but, I mark my life and identity as Before Hiking Big Mountain and After Hiking Big Mountain.

After that experience, I knew there were some big changes that I wanted to make. I wanted to be the kind of person who embraced a physical challenge, who walked through the wilderness, and who breathed deeply on a regular basis. I wanted to create spaces in my life where I could disappear into the mountains or float on the lake. There were new identities I wanted to add to my personal network: hiker, explorer, mountain lover, paddle boarder, outdoors woman. It also meant letting go of some of the identities that no longer served me, like city girl and bar fly.

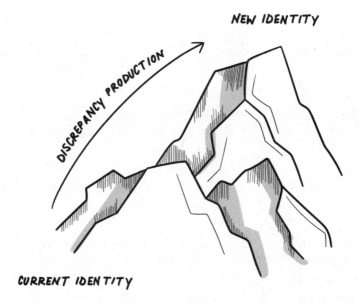

This experience was what Albert Bandura, the psychologist who developed the theory of self-efficacy discussed in Chapter 6, calls "discrepancy production." When I realized that I wanted more-of-this-please on the mountain, I identified the discrepancy between my current identity and an identity I wanted to integrate into my sense of self. Discrepancy production is a key motivating factor for self-regulation and self-directedness. Without that discrepancy, it's hard to chart your course. You charge ahead, ignorant of your destination or what you're likely to encounter along the way. And while continuing to put one proverbial foot in front of the other, you find yourself lost and unmotivated. Bandura writes, "Human self-motivation relies on both *discrepancy production* and *discrepancy reduction*." Discrepancy reduction is the action that we take to shorten the distance between where we're at and what we want. He continues to describe the source of self-motivation, writing, "It requires *proactive control* as well as *reactive control*. People initially motivate themselves through proactive control by setting themselves valued performance standards that create a state of disequilibrium and then mobilizing their effort on the basis of anticipatory estimation of what it would take to reach them."[73] That's a lot to parse—but it's key. So let's parse it.

Bandura's *proactive control* and *valued performance standards* are another way of saying *goal-setting* (or, at least, that's how we can understand it for our purposes). When we decide what we want to work toward and base that on our personal values, we exercise proactive control and set a valued performance standard. Proactive control assumes you feel intrinsic motivation to hike to the summit of your choosing—as opposed to chasing a particular reward or avoiding a negative consequence (i.e., extrinsic motivation). Intrinsic motivation is much more effective for any objective that is strategic, creative, or visionary. While extrinsic motivation (e.g., like a bonus for hitting a pre-set quota) can be motivating for short-term, concrete goals, the kind of growth we're examining here, is much more oriented toward intrinsic motivation.[74] When others set performance standards for us, we generally don't have a real burning desire to meet them. Our jobs, our grades, or the health of our relationships might depend on meeting those standards. This is also true of "borrowing" goals from others. Just because a colleague or a friend climbs a certain mountain doesn't mean you actually want to climb that same mountain—even if the desire to "keep up" is strong. To make long-lasting, transformative change, you've got to care about what you're doing. The thing about a revenue target or sales quota or other quantitative goals is that we rarely care about them enough to make meaningful change. This type of goal can be useful in many settings. But carrot-and-stick goals are unlikely to provide the motivation that serves as the foundation for the work it takes to integrate a new identity into your sense of self. Continuing to unpack Bandura's description of proactive and reactive control, we can examine why setting a valued performance standard (i.e., goal or vision) creates a state of *disequilibrium*. Once you've decided on a change that really means something to you, you can sense the lack of it. You become acutely aware of the distance between you and the goal—the discrepancy that's been produced. This can be uncomfortable, but that's exactly the point. You make yourself uncomfortable in order to figure out how to reach a different version of comfort than the one you currently enjoy. That's the effort you mobilize based on what you think it'll take (anticipatory estimation) to make the desired state real.

As you make that effort, you get feedback—you experience new things, try out new actions, explore possibilities, and receive new information about what it's going to take to meet the valued performance standard you've set. That's the *reactive control* piece. I talk more about this later on. But for now, know that a key part of growth is actually adjusting your plans—not sticking to them.

Now, it's time to take the first big step toward setting your commitments and pursuing what matters. Let's create some discrepancies!

Who Do You Want to Become?

Today, we're bombarded with marketing messages about what we *should* do, be, or want. It's no wonder so many of us feel a lack of motivation—we chase goals that aren't our own. Marketing is designed to produce discrepancies for us. Those discrepancies could be things that share a resemblance to changes you've been considering: trying out some new software or signing up for a meal delivery service. But they can also be discrepancies that you weren't even aware of until the commercial interrupted your video or the ad popped up in your feed. Maybe you had no idea you needed frozen coffee capsules to upgrade your morning brew or that you wanted to invest in crypto. These examples might be relatively benign, but the engine underneath them disrupts our ability to discern what we want for ourselves. And what we want is where any plan, project, or commitment should start.

There have been a number of times in my life where I inadvertently allowed an outside influence to impact major decisions. But one decision, in particular, sticks with me to this day. After college, I was set to pursue a master's degree at my top-choice graduate school. My tuition was completely taken care of, but I'd taken on significant debt to cover living expenses. On top of that, job prospects after graduation were bleak.

Over the summer, between undergrad and starting my graduate program, I started to have second thoughts. I didn't know it at the time, but now I recognize I was burned out after four years of academic and social striving. My resources were exhausted. I didn't have the capacity I needed to navigate my doubt. I started to worry more and more about the future and whether I would ever have a stable career that would pay the bills. These fears were not unfounded, but the specter of poverty amplified my anxiety. On the verge of a nervous breakdown, just two weeks before I was set to start school, I wrote my college advisor an email. I told him I didn't think I could go through with it. He and his wife, another academic, invited me to their house for dinner. They were gentle and gracious, but persistent that I could make it work—school, a career, life. I cried and cried. Thinking about the situation now still fills me with overwhelming emotion. I didn't go to grad school. I abandoned my own vision of who I wanted to become because I succumbed to the message that a stable career was more valuable than pursuing intellectual curiosity.

Years later, I returned to my alma mater as a guest lecturer to share my experience with social media. It felt like a small redemption. When I finally met with my former advisor, whom I'd avoided out of shame ever since that evening, he told me that he and his wife were a bit envious of what I was doing. He said they would love to have the kind of time I was able to devote to writing. That made quite an impression on me. Yes, I'd gotten off course. But I steered my ship back in the direction of who I wanted to become more than I gave myself credit for. I'm not an academic in an institution today—but I do get paid to think, teach, and explore big questions. That's pretty damn cool. I'm grateful to the potency of my original personal vision. Even now, as I write this book, I told my network that I was "on sabbatical" from the usual course of business. I'm knee deep in philosophy and psychology texts. The strength of my vision has kept me motivated to create this life. It's not what I expected to be doing. But today, my experience is completely aligned with a vision I formulated more than 20 years ago.

"Who do you want to become?" is a multidimensional question, and the more often we're willing to engage with it, the more freedom we'll feel from outside sources. Even in a multicultural, secular society, we experience a narrow, hegemonic message about who we're supposed to become. This message is part socialization and part social conditioning. Socialization instills cultural values and beliefs to create continuity. Social conditioning goes further. Conditioning teaches us what are acceptable behaviors and desired outcomes as members of a social group—whether that's a small group like a family or church or a much larger group like a nation. While socialization might instill a cultural value for family, social conditioning might code that value in distinct gender roles within the family. Socialization might instill a value for education, social conditioning might code that value as the need to go to college to major in a field that pays well.

If we take a look at the systems that are examined in Chapter 2, we can see that these systems instill values and encode them in specific behaviors. These systems create social meaning and teach acceptable behaviors with the threat of negative consequences (poverty, damnation, stigmatization) for noncompliance. These aren't the only systems that condition us, of course. Any group we belong to can create social conditioning that changes how we see ourselves and our place in the social order. And our identities and relationship to dominant culture may mean we learn the lessons of social conditioning differently than others do. Social conditioning creates the ladder for us to climb and teaches us who to become, while it obscures our own ideas of how we want to grow. We learn to associate certain behaviors with desired outcomes, so we pursue those outcomes as we perform the behaviors.

Here C. Thi Nguyen, whose philosophy of games is introduced in Chapter 6, provides a structure for deconstructing this process. As I have mentioned, Nguyen offers a framework for "value capture." Value capture, you might remember, is how we are prone to use simplified, quantifiable metrics to stand in for goals that we'd otherwise understand as much more complex and nuanced. Nguyen's framework has three components. The first is that what we value (individually or culturally) is "rich, subtle, and hard-to-express." The second recognizes that simplified metrics help us to communicate those values across platforms and environments, as well as our performance in relation to those values. And the third component of value capture is that these "simplified versions take over in our motivation and deliberation."[75] Social conditioning and value capture go hand in hand. In fact, you might think of social conditioning as value *hijacking*. For example, we might value intimate relationships (a complex and rich value) and, through conditioning, learn that heterosexual marriage is the acceptable expression (simplified metric) of that value. Instead of seeking out intimate relationships in all their rich and subtle possibilities, we spend our twenties looking for the perfect husband or wife (simplified version takes over motivation). Our value for intimacy was hijacked by social conditioning in order to reproduce existing power structures and create a more homogenous society.

PERSONAL RESPONSIBILITY

SELF-DISCIPLINE

INDEPENDENCE

What happens when we reverse this process? Can we reveal how our values get hijacked in the first place? First, we look for the simplified metrics that influence our decision-making and action: go to college, get married, buy a house, have kids, get promoted, and so on. Then, we examine the social or institutional environment that created that expectation: government, media, family, church, and so on. Then we ask what more complex and nuanced values did that environment simplify. Finally, we analyze whether we hold those values and what other ways those values might be expressed. The realization that you've experienced value hijacking through social conditioning has great benefits for you as an individual—but it also has the capacity to transform groups. When you purposefully deconstruct social conditioning for yourself, you find it's much easier to accept choices that are very different from your own. Instead of expecting others' choices to mimic your own, you recognize how rich shared values lead to different expressions of those values. Deconstruction allows us to thrive in diverse and complex groups. We start to see interdependence in our systems instead of the need for self-reliance and individualism.

Before we move on, I recommend you deconstruct one or more of the "shoulds" your conditioning trained you to want. I've previously listed a number of examples that might be on your mind right now. Or, you might consider what perceived shortcomings are riling up your social conditioning. What do you feel you should overcome or change? It could be that you "should" be making more money, hustling more at work, losing weight, getting fit, and so on. Working backward, consider the social or institutional environment that created that "should" for you. Then, consider the value behind that "should" and whether it's a value you actually hold. Have your personal values been hijacked? Finally, if you do hold that value, consider how else you might express it and how expressing it in that way might be more satisfying.

Your Personal Vision

While deconstruction and recovery of hijacked values is a continual process, you can get a snapshot of where you're at right now with it and where you might want to go next. The tool you use to get this snapshot is your personal vision. Your personal vision is where you want to end up 5, 10, or maybe 20 years in the future. Maybe you created a vision board or journaled on your vision in the past. Maybe you spent time daydreaming or meditating about your future. Those are fabulous tools. I encourage you to use those tools—or any creative tool that works for you—as you feel out your vision through the prompts below. While many personal vision exercises will encourage you to come up with lists of milestones or goals you want to have achieved, I recommend something that is less precise. Creating a personal vision is *not* goal-setting. Your vision shouldn't be specific targets you want to hit. Instead, your vision is describing how you want to experience the next phase of your life. Describe how you want to feel as much or more than you describe material conditions. Allow examples of what you want to emerge naturally but hold them loosely. Keep your personal values and what they mean to you in mind as you flesh out your vision.

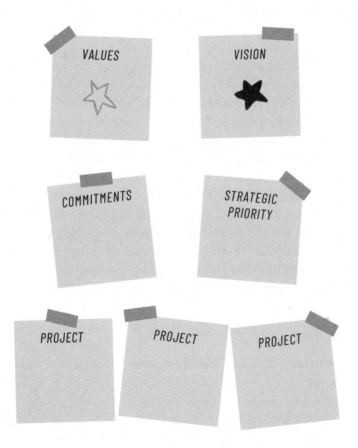

To start, bring to mind a moment of deep satisfaction or transformation, much like my time on Big Mountain. Immerse yourself in this experience whatever it might be. Notice if you feel drawn to a particular aspect of that memory, a new feeling in your body, or a sense of longing. The specifics of the memory aren't terribly important— what's important is getting in the headspace of satisfaction, affirmation, and profound desire. Using whatever creative tool you prefer, record what comes up for you as you consider this memory. What do you notice? What do you feel? What's calling out for you?

From there, consider what you've learned about yourself as a way of creating some distance from those pesky outside influences. What have you learned about yourself this year? What have you learned about yourself since becoming an adult? What have you learned about yourself through your relationships? What have you learned about yourself through your work? These questions should remind you that you're full of self-knowledge as well as self-efficacy. Again, use whatever creative tool is helpful to record what comes up for you.

Next, brainstorm all the ways you feel satisfied with your life and work right now. Even if it's a short list, reminding yourself that there is good *right now* is key to believing you can also create change. Then, consider how you're feeling drawn to grow or evolve. What kind of change is pulling on your right now? Why? What would that kind of change mean for you? At this point, let's acknowledge that there's a constructive tension here. Things can be good *and* we can also want different things. We can feel satisfaction in the present *and* desire for growth. Or, as Sebene Selassie put it in an episode of the Hurry Slowly podcast, "We don't have to make ourselves a problem to aspire to transformation."[76]

Now, you can move on to considering the different dimensions of your personal vision.

Naming Your Vision

Given the potential growth and change you just explored, start to imagine what you want for yourself, say, 10 years from now. In 10 years, a lot can happen. Your life—as well as your experience of it—can change drastically. So really nothing is off limits as you visualize your future. And because we're focused as much on feelings and experience as we are the specifics of what you might want, even seemingly absurd desires can tell you quite a bit about how you want to grow.

Now, a word of caution: You do not need to know how to accomplish this future you're starting to envision. While that might seem obvious, lots of folks get stuck here. We limit ourselves and our desires because we want them to be "realistic" and assume that "realistic" means there's a clear-cut path to your destination. I cannot stress enough that "how" can only be learned once the "what" is established. You are capable of figuring so much out on your own and with others. And the fact that you haven't figured out how to get what you want to this point does not mean it's impossible. It means that you haven't fully conceived of what you want in order to set about learning how to make it happen. It's quite difficult to solve a problem when the problem hasn't been stated, right?

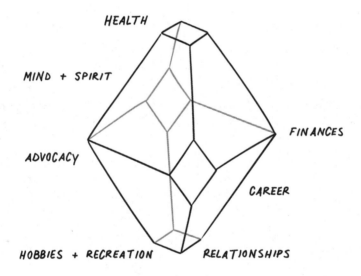

As I have mentioned earlier, your personal vision is multidimen-sional (i.e., health, work, finances, advocacy, etc.). Every dimension matters, and in some dimensions, you might find that your vision is easier to access. In other dimensions, you might find it's a challenge to know what you really want. In that case, consider how what seems clearer tells you about dimensions that seem fuzzy. Within each dimension, explore three aspects: how you want to feel, what you want to experience, and what material conditions you desire. When you think about how you want to feel, let your body do the talking. What physical sensations come up for you when you consider your future? Past the anxiety that might come from thinking about the discrepancy between now and then, what emotions do you connect to these sensations? When you think about what you want to experience, consider the quality of your future experiences. Are you looking for adventure? Peace? Mastery? Coziness? And finally, when you consider the material conditions of your future, allow yourself to think through some specifics. Here, you might name a new career, new members of your family, a new financial situation, or a new way of using your passion to support a cause you care about. These specifics help you further home in on how you want to feel and what you want to experience.

Use the following questions to outline your personal vision. Feel free to use whatever tools are helpful to you: drawing, collage, music, dance, meditation, journaling, conversation. But do find a way to record your findings so your personal vision can continue to guide you through this process.

Exercise:

- What do you want for your relationships?
- What do you want for your health?
- What do you want for your mind and spirit?
- What do you want for your finances?
- What do you want for your work?
- What do you want for your advocacy or impact in the world?
- What do you want for your recreation or hobbies?

The Growth Edge

Years before my transformative experience on the Big Mountain trail, I heard about a hike in neighboring Glacier National Park. It's called the Highline Trail, and it's visible from the iconic Going-to-the Sun Road that cuts east-west through the southern third of the park over the continental divide. From the safety of an earlier car ride on the road, my husband and mother-in-law pointed out the trail, as well as the tiny people on it. It's cut right into the side of the mountain. They told me that the trail in that section is four- to six-feet wide and that there was a chain to hold onto on the mountain side but no barrier on the valley side, which features a sheer drop of hundreds of feet and a clear view of Lake McDonald a couple of thousand feet below. In other words, this trail is not for the faint of heart or those with a fear of heights.

When I first heard about the Highline Trail, I could not imagine myself on that trail. I was not that kind of person. But once I started to shed some of the conditioning that I'd grown up with and create a vision for who I wanted to become, I hungered for the challenge of the Highline Trail. The next year, as I considered the projects I wanted to accomplish, I put hiking the Highline on my list. Our summer trip out to Montana came and went and, while I enjoyed some great hiking, we didn't take on the Highline Trail. The next year, as another retreat group visited the park, a couple of our participants wanted to see what the hype was all about. We walked through the alpine meadow at the trailhead until we reached the rock face—and the beginning of the scary section. One of the participants, Mark, walked out onto the trail. My stomach was in my throat. I desperately wanted to experience that trail, that feeling of being perched on a ledge overlooking the world, but I was so scared of heights. "Come on, Tara. It's fine," Mark beckoned me. And I did. We didn't have time to complete the hike (it's 13 miles long), but we did get a good feel for that stretch of trail. The next year, we vowed to hike it as a group. And lo and behold, the day before the next retreat started, a small group set out on the Highline Trail. Thinking back on that experience, I reconnect with the same joy I felt on Big Mountain. The Highline was a growth edge for me—and meeting and exceeding that growth edge, not because I had something to prove but because I really truly wanted that experience, felt like a huge milestone in creating the life I want for myself.

A growth edge is a perceived limitation (not a real limitation) that you identify as a focus for growth. My growth edge on the Highline was a fear of heights and a lack of willingness to push myself physically. At the point I finally completed the trail, I'd already started climbing and had run a half-marathon—so I'd tested that growth edge already. But the experience itself allowed me to really integrate a new identity and an expansion of what I believed I was capable of. Challenging a growth edge is profoundly meaningful whether it culminates in a one-time experience like mine or becomes a habit. No doubt, working toward your personal vision will give you plenty of growth edges to explore.

Your growth edges will often express themselves as can'ts, don'ts, and shouldn'ts. They voice themselves in limiting beliefs and logical reasoning. They surface from the never-ending loops we seem to regularly find ourselves in. You may not be able to tell a growth edge from a true limitation until you start to test it. If you notice a true limitation, you might feel disappointment or even grief. When you recognize that limitation, though, you have an opportunity to process the feelings that come with it. It may not be easy, but it's worth it. You put yourself in a better place to envision new ways of creating what you want without transgressing that hard line when you take the time to process the emotions associated with it.

When you challenge a growth edge, you change. It might happen slowly, but when you wear away at your growth edge, you become someone new. Before I hiked the Highline, I *couldn't* hike a 13-mile trail. I *couldn't* be up that high without a solid barrier. But little by little, by challenging those growth edges, I learned that I *love* long hikes, steep climbs, and being up above the tree line. I left a different person back at the trailhead and emerged as someone new—and yet more me than ever before. I discovered that endurance, fear of heights, and physical challenge were perceived limitations, rather than actual ones. On the other hand, I've learned that social anxiety and managing people are actual limitations for me—ones I tried long and hard to push through to no avail. We all have different growth edges and actual limitations. Our bodies, brains, access to resources, desires, and past experiences form your particular mix.

Now that you have a clearer vision of your desired future, you can get into the work of identifying what you want to change. That means the triumphant return of the question, "Who do you want to become?" Hopefully, you have a clear and compelling new personal vision. But you're not that person yet. You're not living their life, feeling their feelings, or experiencing what they experience yet. That's good: discrepancy production unlocked. So who *is* this person living in your desired future? How do they think? What do they do on a daily basis? How do they tackle the challenges in front of them? What identities do they hold? What habits or routines do they have?

It's entirely possible that you won't quite recognize the person you envision in this future state. The "you" that's made your vision real might feel like a bit of a stranger. As I've interviewed hundreds of business owners over the years, I've often asked them about the identity crises they've faced. Often, what we might call an identity crisis in the moment isn't so much a *crisis* as it is a recognition that there's someone new looking back at you from the mirror. That person has explored their growth edges, taken note of their limitations, confronted their fear, and examined their desires. They've done things they're really proud of and learned so much about themselves. This is the process of self-actualization.

In the 1943 paper where he first outlined the hierarchy of basic needs, Abraham Maslow pointed to the "restlessness" that is often experienced even after the first four sets of basic needs are met (i.e., physiological, safety, love). This is the desire for *self-actualization*, which Maslow defines as, "the tendency for [a person] to become actualized in what he is potentially. This tendency might be phrased as the desire to become more and more what one is, to become everything that one is capable of becoming."[77] Our personal vision is our current idea—from the limited perspective we hold—of what our potentiality is. We might think of our growth edges as the uncomfortable choices and courses of action we take in the pursuit of fully becoming what we're able to become.

Likely, you see a pretty large discrepancy between who you are now and who you want to become. Who you are now isn't a problem (thanks, Sebene Selassie); you've already put in a lot of work to become this version of yourself. But now, there's the opportunity to actualize this *next* version of you. It's going to take time and practice, though. You'll need to choose what you want to work on first and what can be left for future work. And that's where setting your commitments comes in.

Set Your Commitments

In Chapter 6, goals are differentiated from commitments in terms of achievement and practice. Goals are how we structure an achievement-oriented approach to life. Commitments give us a way to structure a practice-oriented life. Another way to look at this is that goals are results-oriented; commitments are growth-oriented. Goals are future-focused; commitments foster present awareness.

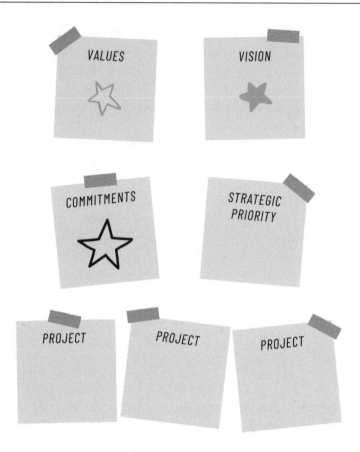

Commitments give us direction for reprogramming our default set of actions—the habits that make up our factory settings. Now, when I say *factory settings* here, I don't mean some transcendent essence of you or a predestined version of your personality that you need to leave behind. I mean the settings that our cultural factory programmed you with and the ways of operating that you've adopted within those settings. It's not that these settings are bad or wrong—just that it's always a good idea to go in there and see if the defaults are actually what you want to be working with. *Confession: One default setting I've started to change on every new app I use is to enlarge the text size. This is how I know I'm getting older.*

It's important to note here how the habits and assumptions that you might want to update once served you. They might have protected you from harm, helped you to navigate unhealthy relationships, or allowed you to cope with school or work. Today, you either no longer need those habits, or you are actively working to change the conditions that necessitated them—freeing you to do things differently.

Take a look at your personal vision. Where do you see the biggest discrepancies between how you operate now and what you envision for the future? Consider how your current habits or assumptions might make this discrepancy feel difficult to overcome. Here are some habits you might look for:

- People-pleasing
- Over-giving
- Hiding
- Disconnecting
- Overfunctioning
- Perfectionism
- Urgency or rushing
- Ignoring boundaries
- Staying silent
- Playing small
- Giving up
- Persisting too long

You might currently operate with assumptions such as your opinion won't be taken seriously, your boundaries won't be respected, you need to prove your love, or you need to do everything yourself. These are the habits and assumptions I've seen most often over the years. Heck, I've experienced most of them myself and am currently working on a handful of them in my own personal growth.

The sheer familiarity and reflexiveness of these habits and assumptions compete with our desire for change. They make it a challenge to see when we could actually choose to do things differently. They convince us that, whatever response is automatically triggered in a situation, it's the natural or common sense response.

Again, consider the discrepancy between your personal vision and how you see yourself today. How does the person you're becoming make different choices about the way you act or think? About the situations you put yourself in? Maybe you notice that the today-you avoids conflict, but the future-you embraces conflict to make your relationships stronger and find a true consensus whenever possible. Maybe you notice that the today-you plays it safe to avoid failure, but the future-you takes risks to do better work. Maybe you notice that the today-you regularly makes choices that lead to burnout, but the future-you prioritizes rest. What habits have kept you stuck in the past? What choices have you made without even thinking about them today? What patterns do you see in your habits and default choices?

A few of these patterns may be self-evident at first glance. Others hide beneath the surface; they take time and practice to spot. Notice when you say things like "can't," "shouldn't," and "don't." Or consider when situations repeat through your personal history like a record skipping. For instance, I notice that I have a burnout cycle that seems to repeat every five years or so. But more than the time, the burnout seems to be caused by overextending myself on emotional labor generally and autistic masking specifically. Now that I've noticed this pattern, I can work to craft solid boundaries and craft better roles for myself to (hopefully) disrupt the cycle.

Now, let's set some commitments. Think of this as a rough draft. You don't need to get these "right"—just jot down the ideas that come up for you as you think through the habits and assumptions you want to work on, the growth edges you want to challenge. Your commitments are your reminders to choose differently instead of going with your default settings. I like to keep my commitments as simple as possible—just two or three words that I can hold in my brain as a reminder to notice when I have the option to take a different action or alter my perspective. Your commitments should apply broadly—from your relationships to work to hobbies to your interior life. And finally, you'll be setting these commitments for a period of at least six months, although a year or more is great, too. Deep growth takes time.

Here some examples of commitments I've used in the past or that others have found useful for their own growth:

- Take rest
- Create energy
- Show up

- Work the system
- Stay the course
- Make room for margin
- Let go
- Get creative
- Simplify
- Choose the risk
- Embrace uncertainty
- Question normal
- Choose vulnerability
- Expect success
- Opt for adventure
- Go big
- Break free
- Accept the invitation

Just like with your personal values, you might start with a long list of ideas and then pare it down to a short list. I recommend choosing no more than two or three to work on over six to 12 months. Think of your commitments as a compass. When you're feeling lost, stuck in a rut, or disoriented, your commitments can get you back on course. They are as useful for tiny everyday choices as they are for life-changing ones.

Once you've found two or three commitments you like, consider a recent situation in which you wish you had done something differently. It could be a fight with a friend or spouse, a project you wish you would have said no to, or an email you responded to out of fear. How would one or more of your commitments have helped you behave like the person you're becoming? The goal, of course, isn't to judge yourself and your actions in the moment. Instead, this is an opportunity to notice how your commitments can provide meaningful direction when you need it most. By identifying how you could have done things differently, you prepare to do things differently in the future.

Now that you've set your commitments (or at least have a rough draft), take them for a spin! Try them out for a week or two before fully committing. What do you learn with those commitments as a guide? While your commitments give you overall directional guidance—like a compass, your *strategy* gives you a map of how to get from point A to point B. And that's what we tackle in Chapter 8.

Exercise:

Using the list on the previous page or creating your own, name two to three commitments you can use to guide your daily actions. These commitments should be widely applicable and guide you in questioning old habits as well as in exploring growth edges.

How would your commitments have guided you to take different action during a recent experience?

8

Choosing Your Direction

Since we do not succeed in fleeing it, let us therefore try to look the truth in the face. Let us try to assume our fundamental ambiguity. It is in the knowledge of the genuine conditions of our life that we must draw our strength to live and our reason for acting.

— Simone de Beauvoir, *The Ethics of Ambiguity*[78]

THERE'S A TRAIL system I love to hike outside of Kalispell, Montana. It's not a big draw like Glacier National Park is. If you're just visiting, you'd never even know that it's there. The trail system is unassuming, located in a small county park. But the terrain is exactly what I love about being outdoors in Montana—quiet, dry, and full of tamaracks. Plus, I can "choose my own adventure" with the trails to create exactly the hike I'm looking for. The only issue is that my mother-in-law told me to be wary of mountain lions a couple of years ago, and I'm still not over that.

The trailhead overlooks a small equestrian center, and the trail itself skirts its edges to start. Down the trail a couple hundred yards, right where the grassy field gives way to the woods, I confront my first choice. I can stay low on the Family Trail, or I can start making my way to the view on the Notch Trail. I choose the Notch Trail—a winding single-track with a moderate elevation gain. The trail leads me up to a few hundred feet from the overlook—at which point, I have a couple of options. Stay on the Notch Trail, or go left or right on the Overlook Trail. I always choose the one that feels like it will not have a black bear or mountain lion waiting for me. So far, I've never been wrong.

The south-side overlook gives me a clear view of the city of Kalispell and, beyond it, Flathead Lake. The north-side overlook gives me a view of Foys Lake and the Whitefish Range of the Rockies. Once I'm done at the top, I have new options. I can go back the way I came, of course, but I prefer to change it up. So I go back by way of the Plum Creek Road Trail. It's actually a logging road, and the trail is wide, less technical than the Notch Trail. From the Plum Creek Road Trail, I take the Family Trail to the Direct Trail back to the trailhead. Round-trip is about four miles.

The reason I wanted to share my favorite "daily hike" trail system with you is because it illustrates an important point: There is rarely a direct path to your vision. Instead, you go from trail to trail as you make your way toward what you want for yourself and your work. That much might seem obvious, but what is likely less clear is that there are a multitude of ways you can traverse those trails and still end up where you want to be. For instance, I don't have to start on the Notch Trail. I could start on the Direct Trail or on Plum Creek Road Trail. I could follow the trail system extension after I hit the overlook and keep climbing before I start downhill. It all depends on my mood, the experience I'm after, who I'm with, even weather conditions or whether I remembered to bring bear spray.

When I'm hiking, my desire is pretty clear and, therefore, so are my choices. It's not hard to know whether I should choose the more difficult trail or add on a few more miles at the top. What I care about is evident to me in that moment. My ability to act on my desires might be constrained by time or weather but even that is clarity I can use to make choices in the moment. The wider world offers much less clarity and far more choices. What we care about is also unclear—or at the least, what we care about is full of contradictions. As I've deconstructed

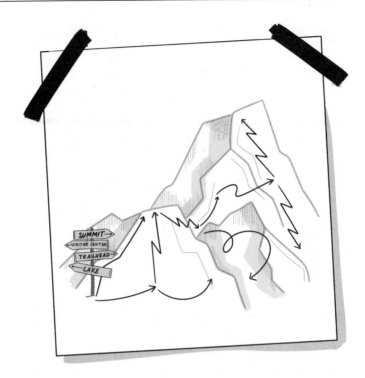

the moral systems we operate in—rugged individualism, Protestant work ethic, supremacy culture, and so on—you might have noticed how these moral systems promote a course of action that might not line up with your personal values or vision. Yet, you know that conforming to these systems makes life easier and more comfortable in many ways. Given those contradictions, what's the right choice? When you're at one of life's trail crossings, how do you choose which way to go?

In all the confusion, we tend to get so fixated on how to make the right choice that we fail to make any choice. When we don't choose, we end up spreading our resources across many different courses of action. We end up overcommitting our resources and undercommitting to our responsibilities or projects. We learn little about what we do actually care about or need in a given situation and what action might be an effective way to get it. To avoid the spiral into overcommitment, you need a strategy.

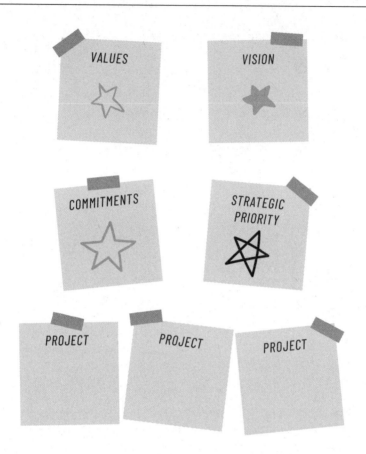

Simply put, a strategy is your designated focus for a period of time. When you have set a strategy, you choose what to let go of—not forever, just for now. Your strategy is a decision about which way you'll take to get from one trail crossing to the next—not how you'll get to where you ultimately want to be. Setting a strategy simplifies what you care about and clarifies what's valuable to you for a given period of time.

For practical reasons, you might realize that your current job or family situation might require a strong work ethic in a way that necessitates a compromise on your personal values. Not in a way that is ethically strained but as a matter of utility. For instance, you might have a boatload of student debt. That debt burden leads you to set a strategy of paying off that debt with a side hustle, which is a drain on your time resources. Is it ideal? No. I believe higher education is a public good that shouldn't result in life-changing debt. But that's not the world we live in. You decide that paying off that debt is more important to you than the personal value you have for adventure that would lead you to, say, solo hiking the Pacific Crest Trail (PCT) with no source of income for six months.

It's not an ethical or moral compromise to delay hiking the PCT. You recognize that the delay serves the purpose of meeting an obligation you have to your credit history because of the system you live in. You recognize that the obligation (in this case, student debt) is a construct of the system, but commit to meeting that obligation sooner rather than later so that more doors are open to you later on.

What I love about strategy is that it dramatically clarifies objectives and lowers the stakes. Yes, the strategy you choose is important but it's not make or break. If you focus on a particular strategy for a year, you've not thrown away the potential to set other strategies in the future. So while you're fiercely committed to the strategy you choose, you can also relax. Fiercely committed and relaxed? That sounds good to me. Instead of anxiously wondering if you'll ever be able to hike the PCT, you know that the action you take now will make it possible.

While commitments give you a framework for growth through daily action, your strategy sets your direction. To go back to the hiking metaphor, my commitment is essentially putting one foot in front of the other. My strategy is the choice of trail and the outcome it leads me to. How do I choose? Well, I need a map. If I just set out on a trail without having an idea where it goes, I *might* eventually get where I was hoping to go, but I'm likely to end up miles away.

Make Your Map

Consider where you're at now and the personal vision you hope to create for yourself. What are some of the different experiences and projects that are going to come up along the way? These experiences and projects are like trailer markers; they help you determine the different options you have as you plot your course. When I make my map, I tend to work backward. I find that constructing the journey in reverse gives me a way to ensure that I work toward my end goal.

But before we go any further, we need to focus in. You can apply strategy and map-making to any area of your vision but I don't recommend making a map that incorporates your *entire* vision. It will be full of far too many assumptions and missing information. So the first bit of strategy work we do is to choose a particular area to work on. For many, this will be work or family; for others, it might be finances or advocacy. What area you choose only matters in that it determines what you'll see concrete progress on first. To that end, if there is a particular area that you need to create change in order to get healthy or feel more stable, choose that one. If a more sustainable financial situation, or career change, or political engagement would lead to the conditions that make other changes more manageable, start there.

I'll share an example to give you a feel for this process. A few years ago, my husband and I decided to start a podcast production agency after we spotted an opportunity in the market. We knew we could build on my own success in podcasting and bring a new level of production and content strategy for podcasts to business owners. We also knew that we wanted to build a company that we could eventually exit. Our shared personal vision is that our work revolves around our intellectual and creative pursuits, rather than working for or with others. So that was the ultimate destination to which we wanted to make a map.

Working backward, we considered what would need to be in place to sell a company. There are two key things: a strong book of clients and a proven, profitable system. Fulfilling those two requirements would be the penultimate trail crossing, so we could step back and consider what we might need to do to put those things in place. We'd need strong documentation and efficient processes as well as a pricing framework that paid all labor plus profit. We'd also need a staff that could produce podcasts without our direct management so that we could develop a large enough client base to make the business attractive to a buyer. Because a strong system and profitable pricing makes it *much* easier to staff up and increase capacity, we knew the next step down the trail was hiring and training. (Remember, we're mapping this out backward.) That meant our strategic development needed to start with building the system and finding the right pricing. With that decision made, we could break that strategy down into projects.

Setting strategy is like that old adage about eating an elephant one bite at a time. When you consider your personal vision overall, it's easy to be overwhelmed by the idea of everything you want to do or change.

You freeze up and don't do anything; or, you try out a bunch of small experiments that don't lead to meaningful results. Your strategy focuses on a particular direction you want to see progress in and helps you create a plan for compounding growth. Here's how the process unfolds:

- Choose an area of your personal vision you want to work on.
- Identify the change you want to make or outcome you want to create. This doesn't have to be super specific, just identifiable and meaningful.
- Consider what you'll need to do immediately before you realize that change or outcome. There may be multiple pieces to put in place.
- Take a step back and consider what you'll need to do immediately before *that*.
- Repeat the process of stepping back and recording what all needs to be in place to create the piece you just identified until you reach something that feels like your current reality.

Once you've mapped out those different points, you connect them with trails. Think of this more like a flowchart than a linear path. What are all the different places you could start? Once you complete that trail, what are your options? Again, repeat the process until you have a map of the different paths you could take to create your vision.

The last question (for now) is: *Where do you want to start?*

Be gentle with yourself. Maybe it seems like there are no good options. Or maybe it seems like they're *all* good options, and you'd hate to miss out on any of them. Remember, strategy doesn't deny you opportunities. Strategy allows you to order your progress and focus on one thing at a time. Again, if there's a place to start that will provide for more stability or well-being, start there. If you're in a good place already, it's up to you and what you're most curious about.

Once you've decided which way you'll take at the trailhead, you might discover that your map needs some adjustments. As you move along, you gather new information and come upon other options that aren't on your map. Unlike a map for hiking, your trail map can always be adjusted as you learn and grow. So don't hesitate to update it as you make progress.

To finish off your map, name the first trail you'll embark on—that's your strategic priority. Your strategic priority is the jumping off point that helps you identify the projects you'll choose to work on, as well as the projects you'll put on the back burner. While your commitments help you choose the best course of action on a daily basis, your strategic priorities help you identify the longer-term investments you want to make in your growth and change.

Consider the trail you've chosen to embark on first and then reflect on what habits, routines, or systems need to adjust as you travel toward the next trail junction. Notice if there are any patterns that seem familiar or whether there's any overlap with another trail on your map. For instance, maybe your first trail is to prioritize your own needs. You notice that you have a habit of making sure everyone else is taken care of first—and you do this at home, at work, and even at the grocery store. At this point, you might not even know what your needs are (that's certainly something I struggle with). So you might decide that your first strategic priority is going to be to identify your needs and meet them. Just like with your commitments, your strategic priorities will be fairly broad. We're setting a course—not setting goals. We'll make it more actionable when we consider the projects you'll tackle to make it happen.

Wanting to Change Is Only the First Step

Imagine what six months or a year spent focused identifying your needs and meeting them would do for you. Imagine the other changes that might catalyze. Think about how you would feel different at the end of that period and the habits you'd learn to take with you as you continue on your journey. Of course, if it were as simple as just setting off down a trail, you'd have already done it by now. Change is hard—for so many reasons. Remember psychologist Robert Kegan who formulated the constructive developmental theory of psychology? Well, Kegan, along with Lisa Lahey, also studied why change is so difficult. Together, they created the immunity to change framework. What they discovered is that the reason it's so hard to make a change you genuinely want to make is that beneath that desire for change there's a competing commitment. There is something else that we're *more* committed to than the change we want to make.[79]

Not long ago, I needed to change my work in a big way due to my health. While the course of action was crystal clear, I couldn't proceed for months because I had a competing commitment. I was committed to the appearance of success, like I didn't struggle at all. The idea of taking action that defied that carefully constructed public version of me brought me to my knees. My desire to appear invincible made me sicker than I already was. It took some difficult conversations with my therapist to identify this competing commitment and actually make a change.

The process doesn't stop when you identify the competing commitment, though. The next step is to examine why that commitment exists and why it's so important to you. That's what Kegan and Lahey call the "big assumption." For me, the big assumption was that people would think less of me and abandon me if I admitted my struggle. And for that reason, I didn't respect my own needs or pursue the strategic action that I needed to take. As I admitted this fear and talked it through with my therapist and the rest of my support team, I was able to replace that big assumption, ease the competing commitment, and take the needed action.

BIG ASSUMPTION
COMPETING COMMITMENT

Kegan and Lahey explain, "Big assumptions reflect the very human manner in which we invent or shape a picture of the world and then take our inventions for reality." They suggest a four-step process for unpacking a big assumption. First, notice your current behavior. How does the way you behave today reflect or reinforce the big assumption? Second, explore evidence that contradicts your big assumption. Confirmation bias is tough to overcome—if you want to continue believing your big assumption, you'll find plenty of examples of why it's true. So you have to go out looking for evidence to the contrary. What stories or experiences (your own or others') show how your big assumption is false? Third, trace the history of your big assumption. Big assumptions are a method of sense-making—albeit an imperfect one. We form these stories about The Way Things Are as an attempt to make sense of events or experiences. If you dig into the experiences that you were trying to make sense of as you formed those assumptions, you can identify how that assumption served you in the past—and why it's getting in the way now. Finally, Kegan and Lahey recommend testing the assumption. How could you behave counter to your big assumption to prove it false? Can you try out a low-stakes version of the bigger change you're looking to make as an experiment? Starting to rewrite your big assumption by playing outside its boundaries in a less risky way will give you confidence to follow-through on your commitment to bigger change. Be sure to take time to follow this step by processing the results of your experiment. What did you learn? How did it feel? What were the concrete outcomes? Processing the results gives you a way to integrate and make sense of the new information.

It's our immunity to change that makes it so important to pick a trail and stick to it. It might seem like you could tackle a few different trails at once (forget the physics of that for a moment). How difficult is it to identify and prioritize your needs, after all? Or how hard could it be to pursue a promotion? Or what kind of challenge is spending more time with your family? But inherent in the desire to change are all of your competing commitments. For instance, if you're more committed to making other people feel at ease than you are to prioritizing your own ease, you'll continue to ignore your own needs. If staying silent in meetings for fear of rejection is more important to you than getting noticed, you'll continue to miss out on promotions. If responding to work emails after hours is what you're really committed to, you'll miss out on quality time with your family. And of course, underneath each of these competing commitments are the assumptions you've used to make sense of past experiences. Maybe ignoring your own needs was a way to maintain the peace during your childhood. Maybe staying silent has been a way to avoid being shut down or called out by people who don't value your opinion. Maybe the fear of what happens if you miss an email or make a mistake gave you the impression that being a bit distracted at home was a good trade-off.

Limit the strategic priority you choose to pursue. Don't set out on a 10-mile hike while also learning to dance and composing a poem. Give yourself permission to take it slow and go deep with whatever you choose to pursue.

Pursuing a Strategy is Practice

In Chapter 4, I examine the role of practice in life and work. Strategy requires practice-orientation. While strategy should have a strong sense of direction and progress, it's also firmly rooted in daily choices and experiments. It takes time and patience to notice competing commitments, narrow your focus, and try something different. And anything that requires time and patience is profoundly countercultural in a society that values speed and efficiency. There's a deep recognition of your own agency embedded within the pursuit of a strategy. When you invest yourself in your choice of strategy, you choose to ignore all of the shoulds and supposed-tos that are thrust on you from the outside world—the marketing messages, the social hierarchies, the short-term benefits. At first, exercising your agency will be an active, conscious practice. If that seems daunting right now, I get it. I really do. But the thing about practice is that, over time, the practice weaves its way into your subconscious. It informs your choices and actions without your active intervention. Your strategy becomes a part of who you are and how you relate to the world. And so, major growth arrives without fanfare.

adrienne maree brown, who reminded us that we need not *assume* misery is required for satisfaction, is a major influence to me on strategic change and growth. brown advocates for what she calls "emergent strategy," an organic practice of noticing, relating, and adapting in exceedingly uncertain circumstances. She writes, "Adapting allows you to know and name current needs and capacity, to be in relationship in real time, as opposed to any cycle of wishing and/or resenting what others do or don't give you."[80] Adaptation is also practice. When we adapt, we exercise our agency. And that brings us back to strategy. While strategy requires focus and commitment, it is not inflexible. Strategy is adaptive. Adaptation is strategic. There is something to learn in every step on the path.

9

Buying In

. . .the practice of freedom—i.e., the morning after, and the morning after that—is what, if we're lucky, takes up most of our waking lives.
— Maggie Nelson, *On Freedom*[81]

WHEN WAS THE last time you worked on something that was really, truly important to you? Something that held a greater meaning for you than it might for someone else? Something that doesn't merely prevent pain, hassle, or misfortune, but something that adds real value to your life? I hope that the last time you engaged in this kind of project was recent—maybe even today. But with the many external demands on your time and attention, it might be difficult to remember. The relentless pace of our culture requires that we continuously react to circumstances beyond our control. We frenetically switch between tasks to convince ourselves we've got it all under control. We shoulder the burden of fixing "problems" and taking on new responsibilities. So much so, that we attempt to stave off reacting by pre-reacting— considering what could go wrong and acting to prevent that. I viscerally feel the absence of a safety net and work to weave one for myself every day, often subverting my commitment to longer-term action in the process. No wonder it can be such a challenge to spend time on meaningful projects or take a longer-term view.

Meaningful projects and long-term action rarely lend themselves to efficiency or optimization. And because economically and culturally we value efficiency and optimization ("Remember, time is money"), we tend to view what we can't do quickly as a luxury. Chapter 2 looks at the cultural systems that have influenced this—rugged individualism, neoliberalism, Protestant work ethic, and supremacy culture. But before you can learn to prioritize meaningful, long-term projects, I want you to look at an unexpected weapon wielded by these cultural systems: time.

Social theorist Barbara Adam explores the quality and instrumentation of time throughout her work. She notes the difference between time as we experience it—day and night, seasons, relationships, conversations—and clock time—hours, minutes, days, weeks. The invention and standardization of clock time facilitated industrial standardization. Once time became a ubiquitous quantitative measurement, it could be used to measure all sorts of processes and actions. We owe all of our modern conceptions of productivity and management to the advent of standardized clock time. As Adam explains, the necessary result of this process is "time compression," trying to fit more into less time. Time compression brings with it an intensified workload. As we fit more and more into less time, we're quite literally working harder, despite the technology that purports to ease our burden. Adam also argues that because time becomes inextricably linked to money, any time off takes on the quality of wasted money. Urgency grips us at work—but also at play and at "rest."[82]

Our pervasive sense of urgency leads to a sense of separation. We feel like the whole world is on our shoulders. We sometimes buckle under the responsibility to keep up and keep smiling. With each of us in our own little bubbles of urgency, we end up distanced from our colleagues, friends, and family. But we also find ourselves separated from our own pleasure and satisfaction, alienated from meaning and purpose. Meditation teacher Sebene Selassie describes what happens as a result: "our lives become about the struggle to keep up." She continues, "To truly feel our experience with depth and presence, we would have to slow down a lot (which would make us less efficient consumers, students, workers, prisoners, soldiers. . .)."[83]

While there are urgent challenges in both our micro and macro worlds today, embodying persistent, unyielding urgency will not help us solve them. But it will make us more susceptible to manipulation, outside influence, and control. When we're just struggling to keep up, it's nearly impossible to think critically about what we're trying to keep up with. As we fight to maintain our pace, we choose action that prioritizes short-term comfort over long-term satisfaction and meaning. We end up caught in The Validation Spiral, divvying out limited resources to more and more (mostly) invented responsibilities.

No matter how much your vision of who you want to become lines up with a picture of traditional Western capitalist success, I sincerely doubt that it includes needless urgency. Your vision isn't about keeping up with or reacting to the external environment. So we need a way to constitute this slower pace and more thoughtful approach—even as we work to detach ourselves from urgency and reactivity. When sharing the difference between practice and achievement in Chapter 4, I introduce you to Kieran Setiya and his book, *Midlife: A Philosophical Guide*, and I explore the role of telic and atelic activities in our lives. Now, I want to draw on a similar duality he shares as a source of dissatisfaction as we age: activities with ameliorative value and activities with existential value.

Activities with ameliorative value are those that prevent something bad from happening or occur in response to something bad happening. For instance, you begrudgingly pull together your paperwork for your accountant so they can do your taxes to avoid the pain of notices (or worse) from the IRS. Or, you take a shower before you go to work so that you don't get a reputation for being unkempt. Or, you make sure your kid did all their homework so that you don't have to deal with an email from the teacher. Granted, there are probably positive reasons you do these things, too. Maybe you get your refund faster or enjoy the smell of your soap or find meaning in helping with school work. But, for many people, these tasks are more ameliorative than they are meaningful on their own. For instance, you could likely be a part of your kid's education without checking up on their homework every evening. You check up on the homework to avoid hassle later on—for both them and you.

Activities with existential value, on the other hand, are the ones you do because they are personally meaningful to you. You don't do them to avoid pain; you do them because the activities create satisfaction all on their own. Reading, baking, and going for long walks while listening to podcasts are activities with existential value for me. I do them because I find joy in them—even when they're challenging or mundane.

Many of the goals we set are ameliorative themselves. Maybe you set a goal to exercise more because if "you don't use it, you lose it." Or maybe you want to spend more time with your family because you worry about getting into fights with your partner. Maybe you want to put down your devices more often because you're trying to avoid the onslaught of daily bad news. How likely are you to stay committed to a goal that's ameliorative? Well, depending on what research you look at, somewhere between 7 percent and 25 percent of people stick with their New Year's resolutions—often our most ameliorative goals. So I'd say the odds aren't good.

Buying In

To follow through on our intentions for growth and change, we need existential commitments. Existential commitments cultivate what I refer to as buy-in. Buy-in is the feeling that you get when you know that what you're working on really, really matters. It's not just busywork, nor is it something you slog through to avoid consequences. It's also not a project you dreamed up with the hope to alleviate phantom discomfort. Buy-in comes from activities that are fundamental to the overall success of your vision.

Buy-in replaces the morally weighty concept of "self-discipline." You don't force yourself to do what needs to be done. You don't deprive yourself or punish yourself. Instead, you create the conditions in which you readily do what you want to do. Importantly, buy-in isn't something you have or you don't. You create buy-in.

I think it's valuable to return to Max Weber and his work on connecting the Protestant work ethic to the spirit of capitalism here. One of Weber's most salient points about the Protestant work ethic was how the culture it created valued work above pleasure, going so far as to declare an ascetic life to be the morally virtuous life. He writes, "In fact, the summum bonum of this ethic, the earning of more and more money, combined with the strict avoidance of all spontaneous enjoyment of life, is above all completely devoid of any eudæmonistic, not to say hedonistic, admixture." To put that in modern terms, Weber concludes that the most virtuous and morally righteous people, according to Puritanical culture, were those who avoided pleasure and enjoyment so as to work harder and earn more money. Importantly, the religious beliefs foundational to this culture inculcated work ethic as a measure of morality and faithfulness. Either you were righteous and self-disciplined or you were born lacking the necessary discipline that would signal your salvation.[84]

Recall Kegan and Lahey's work on our immunity to change. One of the big assumptions I often uncover when working with business owners around growth and mindset is that they believe they aren't the kind of people who are self-disciplined or capable of follow-through. Like they were born with a personal deficiency. This assumption can form for any number of reasons: a teacher told them they were lazy; a parent disciplined them for not doing their homework; the media told them that if they hadn't accomplished X, Y, or Z by the age of 30, they were failing; and so on. And this assumption—this identity—is particularly hard to unravel because it gets reinforced over and over again through culture. In contrast, we're often fed the *opposite* line: You can do anything, don't quit, no limits, and so on. These phrases sound good, but when you are faced with real limitations—and the vast majority of us are—they can be supremely disempowering. Again, we start to internalize that it's our self-discipline that's lacking.

This is where Bandura's concept of self-efficacy can really come in handy for developing buy-in. Remember that self-efficacy is believing that you are capable of the action you want to take to achieve a certain outcome. Actively working to strengthen your self-efficacy is a way of rewriting the big assumption that you're not disciplined enough to succeed at what's important to you. Self-efficacy is influenced by personal experience, observed experiences, social feedback, imagined experience, and physical and emotional states. Each of these are variables that we can experiment with to improve our sense of self-efficacy. We can create small experiments that give us new personal experiences to draw from. We can seek out people who have done what we want to do. We can have conversations with others on similar paths or use meditation to integrate new information. None of these things require prolonged self-discipline or major change.

Let Go of Discipline

"Discipline" is presented as a positive character trait. Most often when we talk about discipline, we talk about the ability to will ourselves to do what we don't want to do so that we achieve a desired outcome. We have to be *disciplined* to lose weight. We have to be *disciplined* to start a business. We have to be *disciplined* to write a book. We assume that misery will lead us to the joy of success. I find that whole notion pretty bleak. I don't want to avoid hard work, but do I really need to be miserable to earn my way to joy? No. When we replace discipline with buy-in, we circumvent the assumption of misery. We don't need to do things we don't want to do to achieve a desired result. Instead, because we know exactly why a particular task matters to the big picture, we can connect with a genuine desire to do that task. It might not be pleasurable, but it's intrinsically valuable. Whatever resistance we might still feel teaches us about the nature of our project.

Here, the Christian philosopher Søren Kierkegaard has insights we can use. In his book *The Lily of the Field and the Bird of the Air*, Kierkegaard cites three skills we can learn from lilies and birds: silence, obedience, and joy. Today, those are three words that can mean very different things to different people—and even in Kierkegaard's time (the mid-1800s), they would have had various connotations. But Kierkegaard uses three discourses to expand on each one. Silence is explained as removing the influence of anything that is not God's will—to find a stillness in which our needs and our actions are perfectly aligned with God's will. Kierkegaard writes that obedience is unconditional submission to the will of God. And joy is understood as living in the present without anxiety about the future or the past.[85] Kierkegaard uses overtly Christian language—exploring scripture and concepts like the will of God. But Kierkegaard's work has had profound influence far outside the bounds of the church. Even if the concept of the "will of God" is anathema to you, there is something valuable here. Stick with me. To cultivate buy-in for what we're up to, we must let go of the assumption of misery—and that's what silence, obedience, and joy can shed light on.

Kierkegaard's discourse on silence tracks with the work we've done to deconstruct the economic, political, and cultural narratives we swim in. Our task is to carve out space—as much as possible—for that silence. We need to quiet the voices of "reason" and the false stories we've learned about ourselves, without disconnecting from reality. While positive-thinking gurus might suggest that silence is actually filled with good vibes, I believe silence is actually what results from being able to approach troubling headlines, disappointing results, and, yes, exciting possibilities with objectivity and detachment. Silence gives us the best chance of taking all the information around us and transforming it into meaningful action or choices. Creating the space for silence is what the whole first half of this book has been about.

Now, let's take a closer look at obedience. Obedience might sound a lot like discipline—the will to do the hard or unpleasant thing. But, instead, we can interpret Kierkegaard's obedience as self-trust. Obedience is action that is in line with both who you are and who you are becoming. The lily and bird don't worry about whether they should be like an industrious ant or a playful otter—they are obedient in doing their own thing. All of the worry from the shoulds and supposed-tos we've internalized from external systems and authority is a distraction from our true task—from obedience. Kierkegaard writes about this in terms of necessity:

> "You, too, are of course subject to necessity. God's will is indeed done in any case, so strive to make a virtue of necessity by doing God's will in unconditional obedience. . . .you might truthfully be able to say of yourself: 'I cannot do anything else, I cannot do otherwise.'"

As I read this, this feels familiar. When I told an editor friend of mine that I was writing this book, I told her that I was excited *and* that I knew it was going to be really hard. She told me, "I don't think it's going to be hard for you." This about knocked me over. She didn't mean, as it has been so often said to me, that I was just so [smart, disciplined, well-resourced] that it would be easy. What she meant was that she observed me as being unconditionally obedient to writing. I wouldn't say that I'm a naturally gifted writer or that I always communicate exactly what I want to say. But writing is a necessity for me. There have been times in my adulthood that I've not written, times where I was trying to do or be other things. But those were bad times. They were times full of the misery of doing something I "should" be doing instead of my necessary task. As Kierkegaard puts it: I cannot do anything else, cannot do otherwise, than write. Or as Joan Didion puts it, "I write entirely to find out what I'm thinking, what I'm looking at, what I see and what it means."[86] I don't personally believe we are born with an innate purpose. And I don't believe that I was put on Earth to write. But I've learned that being obedient to the drive to write has helped me to create meaning and purpose in my life. To return to Setiya's framing, writing has existential value for me at the same time that it provides my livelihood.[87]

When I let go of trying to be something other than what I am, I can access the type of joy that Kierkegaard references in his third discourse. Buying in on important work, giving yourself over to it, feels like joy. Maybe not day-at-an-amusement-park style fun, but joyful nonetheless. Even if the work wouldn't feel joyful to someone else, completing a task or working on a project that gets you one tiny step closer to who you're becoming is satisfying. Like many creative people, I've long avoided administrative tasks that are essential to my work. But I've learned to find the joy in these tasks because I am profoundly aware of how they support my ability to do everything else.

Accountability and Motivation

Throughout this chapter so far, I've shared ways that you can reposition the growth in front of you as something you *want* to do, rather than something you *should* do. Once you've shed the shoulds and supposed-tos that add misery to your life, excitement about the task at hand is a short leap. Yet, for as much as I believe this approach works better than any project management software or reminder set-up, or annoying notifications, folks still want to know about accountability. They claim that if they just had someone who holds them accountable to the work they believe they're supposed to be doing, then they'd be more likely to get it done or make the change. They claim that they're "deadline-oriented" and that due dates give them a way to stay on track.

Unfortunately, this just isn't true for anything but the smallest, most concrete tasks.

The way we organize work or track change is important, no doubt. It's especially important for those who experience difficulty with executive functioning. But no amount of deadlines, flashing red notifications, or threats of being held "accountable" are going to matter if you haven't bought into the purpose of the work they remind you to do. I know just how easy it is to disregard a deadline or notification. In their book *Uncommon Accountability*, Brian Moran and Michael Lennington describe the ways we typically use the concept of "accountability." They cite all of its negative connotations in terms of justice and consequences. And then, they detail another way to see accountability: ownership. No one can own my tasks, habits, or creative work other than me. I was first introduced to this in their first book, *The 12 Week Year*, and it has stuck with me ever since. They write, "We either walk our own personal path toward great accountability, or we don't. No one can hold us accountable, only we can hold ourselves accountable."[88] Fair warning: This concept can quickly fly into the territory of rugged individualism and the personal responsibility doctrine. And, in fact, much of *Uncommon Accountability* does draw from that narrative. I certainly don't blame them—that's the audience they're writing for.

But since I've unpacked individualism and personal responsibility already, let me be clear. Redefining *accountability* in terms of ownership is empowering. It does not mean that your success is in your hands alone, or that failure means you're deficient in some way. Ownership—or my preferred term, *buy-in*—is a way of saying, "This is what I'm choosing for me given the information and resources I have right now." When you take ownership, you choose what to focus on, to invest yourself in, to be obedient to, to feel joyful about. The outcome is irrelevant. Ownership, buying in, being accountable to yourself means doing what you've already chosen to do. Changing what you've already chosen to change. Creating what you've already chosen to create. And it's from that mindset that you find joy and satisfaction in doing what it takes to follow through on what you've chosen.

For you, that might include getting yourself set up with an app that helps you plan out your projects. Or it could mean gathering a group of people working on similar projects. You might even check in daily with a friend over email to share your progress. If that's a helpful way to measure your progress so that you can learn and adjust as you go, do it. But know that there is nothing an app or a colleague can threaten you with that will make you do something you don't want to do, something you haven't chosen. No one can hold you accountable but yourself—so you better buy in.

Cultivating Buy-In

Buy-in shifts the objective from checking items off your list to thinking critically about the journey. "What's next?" is only the first (instead of the only) question. When you think critically about your growth or the work at hand, you also consider why you do it, what you learn, and how you can improve on things as you go. No longer a machine executing a list of instructions, you're a human who takes an active interest in the creative challenge of doing the work.

If you're like me, this is kind of work—personal or professional— you crave. And yet, it's the kind of work we are so likely to deny ourselves while we seek out new ways to increase our productivity or maintain the juggling act of everyday life. We might even think we don't deserve this kind of work—that it's the privilege of a certain kind of person with a particular skill set or station in life. But we all deserve the experience of doing work that matters to us—and we all have the opportunity to choose, even in a very small way, to see a bit more of what we do in that light. How can you draw a connection between your daily tasks and your vision for the future? How can you create meaning from the mundane?

Buy-in relies on your active choice to pursue what you want to pursue. Growth, change, creating cool stuff—it all takes some degree of strategic focus. In Chapter 8, you are asked to make a "map" of different paths you'd need to take as you move between your current condition and your personal vision. Now, you must consider the concrete things you'll work on while you're on the path you've chosen to start with. Those are your projects. When your projects are clearly tied to your strategy and your strategy is clearly tied to your vision and your vision is clearly tied to your values, you know that what you're working on really, really matters. You can feel the joy of buy-in. Maybe not every hour of every day. But that feeling is potent. Doing something that really, really matters to you (and to who you are becoming) for even an hour a day can completely change your outlook in the other 23 hours.

So, let's get to work.

Reflection:

- What was the last project you worked on that held existential value for you? Why is it meaningful to you?
- What is something you do regularly for ameliorative value? How else could you approach this activity?
- What do you do not because you "have to" but because it makes you feel more like yourself, obedient to your nature?
- Considering the strategic priority you chose, what activities or projects will you have to establish buy-in for?

10

Planning Projects

I once had a therapist tell me that flexibility without structure isn't flexibility at all; it's just chaos.

— Amanda Montell, *Cultish: The Language of Fanaticism*[89]

MY HUSBAND OFTEN tells me about the projects he's "planning." He plans to grow hops off our side porch, so it can wind its way up to the Juliette balcony above. He's plans to line our backyard fence with mosquito-repellent plants. He has plans to rearrange the living room and make radiator covers from scratch. But when my husband says he's planning, he means he's daydreaming. It took me forever to understand this. Probably because I'm extremely literal. Planning, to me, means research, timeframes, and budgets. For him, though, daydreaming is how he processes what he really wants out of life. It's how he creates his own personal vision.

For others, planning means making a linear list of tasks, putting dates on calendars, and doing their darnedest to see it through. Instead of visionary or strategic, it's super task-oriented. Creating a vision is important. Following through on the work is important (I cover that soon). But these two different ways of approaching "planning" belie a key issue with how the vast majority of us approach projects—both personal and professional. Planning a project is neither creating a vision (or a daydream) nor is it a checklist. A project falls somewhere in the middle. It's a discrete unit of your strategy—the trail you've chosen to travel on. Further, you can plan a project without actually knowing how to complete that project. A project is a container for your daily effort, your tasks, and checklists, but it encompasses a greater period of time and a bigger opportunity to learn.

Projects are like trail markers or landmarks on the trail you're currently on (your strategic priority) to move closer to your vision. They're way-finders that make a long and winding journey a little more precise. Your projects help you measure your progress, ensure you're still on the right path, and provide the opportunity for learning. Projects turn your strategy into concrete action and measurable results. As I said, you don't actually have to know how to complete a project to plan for it, but you should be able to identify specifically how each project will help you move toward your vision.

How do you know what a project is—versus a strategy or a task? There are three factors I use to shape a project. First, projects have a clear scope and outcome. I need to be able to know when the project is complete—or when the project can be moved into an ongoing routine or system. Second, a project typically takes four to eight weeks to complete. If you're only working one project at a time and you have the space to devote significant time or focus to that project, then a project might last only a week or two. But for the average 21st-century human with plenty of varying responsibilities, a project is going to take some time. If you suspect that the project is going to take you much longer than eight weeks to complete, though, you can likely divide it into two or more smaller projects. Finally, projects fulfill your strategy. Each project should have its own purpose—it should mean something to you because you can see how it's connected to your strategy and how your strategy is connected to your vision.

Time to Brainstorm

We created our personal visions, set our strategies, and now we can plan some projects. Before you start thinking about the projects you'll commit to, revisit your personal vision, your commitments, and your strategy. Take a moment to not just *think* about them but to *feel* them in your body. When I connect to my vision, commitments, and strategy, I feel it in my chest and arms. The sensation is adjacent to anxiety—butterflies and tightness—but it's the electricity of excitement. When I think about what I'm planning, I want to cultivate that sensation because it keeps me focused and oriented to what I really want.

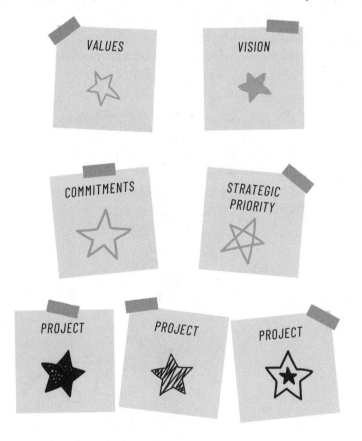

Once you've found those sensations and reconnected with the bigger picture, start brainstorming. What are all the different ways you could work through your strategy? What could you create? What could you learn? What could you experience that would help you move forward strategically?

Let's use my husband again as an example. His vision is to become a full-time artist after we exit our production agency. He knows that becoming a full-time artist doesn't happen overnight, so he's working toward that vision now—even if he doesn't expect it to happen for eight to 10 years. His current strategic priority is exploring different media: charcoal, ink, pencil, fabric, fiber. He's getting a feel for turning ideas into reality using all types of tools. As I write, he's upstairs learning to quilt. Quilting has always interested him but this is the first time he's devoted time to actually learning the craft of it. "Learn how to quilt" is too broad to be a project. It's a process that takes years, not weeks. And, it's open-ended, lacking a clear way to signal completion. Instead, learning how to quilt is many projects. The first project was something he completed last week: one quilt block. That block was the culmination of a few weeks of learning and practice. He had to study how to cut the fabric, arrange it, and use the sewing machine. He also had to practice how to maintain his seam allowances and match his corners. The result? The block looked pretty good! Of course, there's always room for improvement, but his diligence paid off. Now, he's moved on to the next project: hand-piecing. (I had to go upstairs to get the report!)

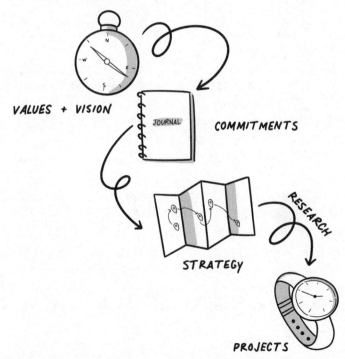

VALUES + VISION

COMMITMENTS

STRATEGY

RESEARCH

PROJECTS

Okay, so maybe brainstorming potential projects is a little open-ended. After all, my husband didn't really know what all he could choose from when he decided to work on quilting. When you're starting in on a new strategy, you'll probably want to do some research. Are there exercises, frameworks, or training plans out there already that would help you move forward with your strategy? Are there people who have done something similar you could talk to? Stories you could read? Classes you could take? Are there community structures that would give you the chance to work on a project alongside others (like running clubs, National Novel Writing Month, or group therapy)? Projects don't have to spring fully formed from your mind to be helpful and meaningful. One of the most meaningful projects I've done recently was to take a creative nonfiction writing class. The class's reading and writing assignments gave structure to a broader, harder-to-quantify strategy for improving as a writer.

Finally, while a day or weekend set aside for planning can be helpful, planning itself is a much more amorphous and fluid task. Your plan will not get figured out on the day and time that you schedule it. So take some time for your list of potential projects to take shape and be open to new ideas coming to you as you go.

Choose Your Projects

Once you have your list of potential projects, you can start to select the ones you'll add to your plan. You might have strong feelings right off the bat—you know exactly what you want to do first or what is going to fit into the capacity you currently have. Or, you might be taking more of a guess. Feeling certain isn't always correlated to "being right." There might be projects that necessarily need to come before other projects. And there might be projects for which you need time to gather additional resources. Or, you might choose an initial project or two to build your self-efficacy for another project that's exciting *and* daunting. The thing to keep in mind is that there is no such thing as "right" when it comes to choosing your projects, as long as you choose projects connected to your larger strategy and vision. Learning halfway through one project that you actually need to start over and do another project first is not a failure. It's not because of some personal deficit. It doesn't mean you're a bad planner. It means you're learning.

Once you have a project or two chosen, be sure those projects fit into the three guidelines for what a project is:

1. Does what you've chosen have a clear scope and outline? How will you know when the project is complete?
2. Do you estimate that this project will take four to eight weeks (adding or subtracting from that time frame depending on your capacity)?
3. Can you connect this project to the strategy you've chosen in some way?

If the answer to any of those questions is "no" or "I don't know," play with the scope, timeframe, and meaning of the project until you can safely answer "yes" to all three questions.

Next Steps

You might be eager to dive into your favorite project management app, crack open your planner, or start making a list. But we should pause and do a little more strategic work before we can get into the "how" of working on your projects. My friend Charlie Gilkey, author of *Start Finishing*, says, "We don't do ideas. We do projects."[90] And right now, your projects are still just ideas. They need clearer form, meaning, and connection to the whole for them to truly make sense.

So take a look at the first project you've chosen. You've already done the gut check on scope, timeframe, and connection to strategy. Now, record that information in a way that increases your buy-in. That's what a Project Brief is for. If you're using this process for a work project, this is probably going to be something you type up and enter into whatever software you use to manage your work. If this is a personal project, your brief might simply belong in your journal or on a Post-it® note. If you're working on this project with other people, say your partner or a team at work, the brief is a document you can share with them to get *their* buy-in, too.

Your Project Brief should answer these key questions:

- How will you know when the project is complete?
- What are you hoping to learn through this project?
- What results are you measuring?
- How long will the project take to complete?
- How does this project help you fulfill your strategy and move closer to your vision?
- What resources (time, money, energy, skill, etc.) are required to complete this project?
- What are the high-level tasks required to complete this project?

Here's an example. Let's say my project is to launch a podcast. I'd create a document of one sort or another that answered each of these questions for that project. And yes, I know that probably sounds like busywork, a bit of overkill. But I assure you that this Project Brief is a valuable document that you'll be grateful you have on a regular basis. So how will I know when this project is complete? Easy. I'll know it's complete when the first episode of the podcast goes live. What am I hoping to learn through this project? I want to research an area of interest by interviewing people about their experiences. What results am I measuring? Well, I could certainly measure downloads or reviews—but what's more important to me are the stories themselves. So I'll be measuring results in terms of people I talk to and episodes I produce. How does this project help me fulfill my strategy and move closer to my vision? I'm doing primary source research on a topic that I want to build expertise in as I gear up for a career change. What resources are required? I'll need to spend money on some new equipment. I'll need time to learn how the production process works. And I'll need relationship resources to get interviews booked. What are the high-level tasks required? Develop the premise of the show. Create a trailer. Book guests. Record interviews. Edit episodes. Get the show listed in directories. And so on. . . .

The Project Brief helps me gather my thoughts, a step we so rarely take the time for. Plus, it gives me a handy reference I can come back to when I'm feeling stuck, disappointed, or just kind of over whatever project I'm working on. It can also help you generate buy-in—for yourself or for others. Please don't skip this step.

Exercise:

Choose your first project and complete a Project Brief:

- How will you know when the project is complete?
- What are you hoping to learn through this project?
- What results are you measuring?
- How long will the project take to complete?
- How does this project help you fulfill your strategy and move closer to your vision?
- What resources (time, money, energy, skill, etc.) are required to complete this project?
- What are the high-level tasks required to complete this project?

Now, let's take a look at some different kinds of projects you might have on your docket.

Closed Loop Projects

A closed loop project is any project that is over and done with once you've completed it. It stands alone. And, you won't be revisiting it again—at least not for a lengthy period of time. Closed loop projects are integral to forwarding your strategy but they aren't being integrated into your regular work once they're finished. Remember telic activities in Chapter 4? Closed loop projects are, essentially, telic activities. The whole point of the project is finishing it so you can move on to the next thing.

Closed loop projects often provide the foundation for another project (or many). Especially when you're pursuing a new strategy, you may have many closed loop projects that need to be completed before you move forward. They're the groundwork for major progress. Closed loop projects might be things like: build a website, create a newsletter, document a system, plan a vacation, and so on.

Open Loop Projects

Open loop projects are similar. They still have a clear scope and endpoint, but they move you forward incrementally. You might not feel quite done when you've completed the project because it's one chunk of your Big Project. A good metaphor here might be going to college. Getting your degree is a Big Project. But you can chunk that down into years, and chunk each year down into semesters. You could even turn each class into a project. When you're done with a class, that project is complete, and (hopefully) you don't ever have to take that class again. But, you still have plenty of *other* classes to take— hence, the open loop.

Open loop projects give you concrete mile markers for bigger projects that are hard to wrap your mind around as a whole. These are often the projects that form when you put a time limit (four to eight weeks) on potential projects. You might realize that the project you first had in mind is more like a six-month project, so you divide it into three eight-week open loop projects.

Routine Projects

A routine project is one that helps you establish a new routine, habit, or system. You work on the project actively and intentionally for a period of time (typically eight to 12 weeks) to establish the routine. Then it becomes part of your regular life or work. You're able to move it from something you need to manage with care to something that's just a part of how you function.

Routine projects build new self-knowledge and reprogram competing commitments that make it difficult to change. They can even add a new dimension to your identity. Routine projects might include things like: writing a weekly newsletter, exercising daily, cooking at home instead of ordering takeout, checking in with your team, making a daily media pitch, and so on.

Don't get hung up on exactly what kind of project you are working on. What's important is that you acknowledge that different kinds of projects serve different functions and help you fulfill your strategy in different ways. Some projects will feel over and done with. Other projects will feel like you're opening a can of worms. And still other projects will come to an end by virtue of the activity fading into the background of everyday life. I offer these distinctions only so that you can see that projects might resolve in various ways.

Make Your Plan

Look, I'm guessing this isn't the first book you've read on planning or productivity. You probably already have some familiarity with your options for planning. Maybe you already have a system that works for you. My intention isn't to reinvent the wheel here. Instead, I want to offer something that most planning and productivity systems don't offer: flexibility. Whether it's vision, strategy, or projects, you don't need to follow my instructions to the letter. You now have a new way to *think* about planning.

From an early age, most of us are programmed to just follow the instructions lest we miss a critical criterion for judgment and see our scores docked. The way you plan—including creating your Project Briefs—is an opportunity to start to reprogram yourself, to see all of your work as creative work, to engage your critical thinking skills in a way that energizes and excites you. Remember that this process is methodically unwinding decades of creative diminishment and personal agency at the hands of institutions or management structures.

What works for me when it comes to planning projects is to break my year down into quarters. I typically have the capacity for three projects per quarter—working simultaneously on each because I like to have different things to do depending on my state of mind. Hence, my projects typically take about 12 weeks instead of four to eight. At the beginning of each year, I very loosely map out what projects will move my strategy forward throughout that year. Then, I assign those projects to the four quarters. At the beginning of each quarter, I reassess what I have planned and complete the Project Briefs for the projects I'll complete in that time. I prefer to have a general idea of what I'll do throughout the year so that I know where I'm headed, but I save the more detailed planning for closer to when it will actually be executed so that I can take what I learn from the past quarter and apply it to the plan.

If you don't know where to start with making your plans, give my process a try. If you have a system that works well for you, or you prefer to plan monthly or plan for sprints, go for it! You're now equipped with a way to think through planning in a way that encourages intentional, sustainable growth and change. But we're not done yet. Because now that you've started to make your plan, the inevitable question is: "Yeah, but how do I stick to my plan?" My answer: don't. I'll explain in the final chapter.

11

Follow-Through, Self-Sabotage, Margin

Where there is hope, there is difficulty.
— Sara Ahmed, *Living a Feminist Life*[91]

AFTER FOUR YEARS of running a few times a week, in 2021, I barely ran at all. I had a nagging pain in my hip that just wouldn't go away. Really, it was a literal pain in the butt. I thought that if I rested it, eventually it would heal itself. Ten months later, I made an appointment with a sports medicine doctor. It turns out, rest was not the answer. She told me that it was tendinosis, an overuse injury that resulted from my hamstring tendon working harder than it should because other muscles didn't do their jobs. After that news, I set about retraining my glutes to fire in different positions so that my hamstring tendon didn't have to work so hard.

The results came relatively quickly—certainly more quickly than taking 10 months off of running. A few months later, I felt like I'd made real progress and could run again. So far, so good! I'm back to building my endurance and running three to four times per week. I'm also lifting weights again—which feels great. The whole last year has been a learning experience, though. Every time I learned something new, I had to adjust my training. At the beginning, the adjustment was to stop running for a while. When that failed to fix anything, I stopped lifting weights and focused on yoga. When I was still in pain after six months of resting, I basically cut back to a long walk each morning. By summer, most of my exercise came while atop my standup paddle board. Working out had become such an important part of my mental health care that the thought of stopping altogether was terrifying. But I knew I couldn't stick with what I'd done for years. Once I talked to the doctor, I had new information, and I could adjust my plans yet again. This time, I knew what I could add back in. I paid attention to signs of improvement so that I could add even more back in. At this point, I'm not back in half-marathon shape, but I'm back to a training plan that feels familiar.

Being a middle-aged athlete has taught me quite a bit about *not* sticking with my plans. I've been in the best shape of my life the last few years, but I'm using a body that's been around the sun 40 times. My joints and ligaments aren't quite as resilient as they once were. If I'm training for a half-marathon and my Achilles tendon starts to act up (as it is prone to do), I know that I need to back off for a bit—and also order new shoes. If it's so cold outside that I can't take a walk without my toes going numb, then I need to reacquaint myself with the treadmill. I listen closely to the feedback my body gives me and adjust. Sounds reasonable, right? Now, full disclosure: Yes, there have been times when I've pushed through an injury when I shouldn't have. There have been times where I stuck with a program when my body was telling me to adjust. But the consequences of those decisions have only made me more committed to adjusting as soon as I notice something is off.

Luckily, the feedback our bodies give us is pretty easy to notice, if we pay attention. The feedback we're most likely to pay attention to is pain. If I feel pain, I look for a cause, assess my activity, and adjust so that I'm not in pain anymore. Our bodies might also produce sensations like exhaustion, pleasure, or queasiness. Again, this is feedback that helps us to make adjustments. Unfortunately, the feedback we receive in other aspects of our lives and work is easier to ignore or miss entirely. We get down on ourselves when a project is falling further and further behind instead of stopping to assess the delays as feedback that warrant a change of plans. We rush ahead with an idea without paying attention to the nagging fear or anxiety in the background that might have something useful to share with us. We're so conditioned to "stick to the plan" that any deviation—no matter how warranted—can feel like a failure.

Every year, people ask me, "How do I make a plan I can stick to?" Everyone wants to know a magic formula to choose goals and make plans they can glue themselves to for a month, a quarter, or a year. They want to avoid the pattern they've repeated over and over again: set a goal, make a plan, start with gusto, and fizzle out after just a few weeks. I don't believe the objective of a plan is to stick to it. A plan is always just a rough draft. Once you've drafted your plan, the goal is to edit it—not publish it. Every day, every week, every month is a chance to learn about yourself and how you'll create your personal vision—or whether the vision you started with is actually what you want in the first place.

So instead of "sticking" to the plan, I advise "working" the plan. While sticking with your plan might mean trying to reach a goal or complete a project and execute it from top to bottom, working your plan means you learn from your early action and make adjustments. While sticking with your plan involves checking every item off your list and hitting all your deadlines, working your plan involves figuring out what to scrap and how long it's really going to take to put all the puzzle pieces together. When you work your plan, you might discover that the objective you're working toward is something totally different than you expected it to be. You might find out that a part of your plan just isn't very important. Or, you might see that there is more learning to be done before the plan can be completed. Every action you take to move forward gives you new information. If you execute the plan as you created it, you miss the opportunity to make your plan better with that information.

New information, adapting your plan, reassessing—it doesn't mean you'll figure out that you have to do *more* to complete your plan. You might. But at least as often, you'll discover that you can do less to achieve the outcome you want. Or, you can do something differently. Or, you might find you need to take a different direction entirely. One of the reasons we don't see our plans this way—as a rough draft, a learning process—is because we're trying to "get it right." We're trying to follow a perceived set of instructions to the letter. But there truly is no set of instructions, no manual for how to create what you want to create. For every step of the plan, there is only ever your best guess based on what you know at that moment. This is liberating.

Now before all the productivity hackers and planning gurus come at me, I realize that no one literally tells you to stick to your plan if new information comes to light. But what is said isn't always what's done or what's internalized. That's why it's so important to be explicit when it comes to making your planning process a learning process.

Planning as a Feedback Loop

Creating a plan creates the opportunity to gather feedback. Feedback as in data, not as in criticism. Planning, in essence, says "This is how I expect things to go down." If you plow ahead without that initial expectation, you don't have a baseline to measure your results. You miss out on the information you could gather by comparing what you *thought* would happen to what *actually* happened. Now, if you've been burned by goal-setting or planning in the past, you might try to avoid that comparison altogether. Past failure is one of the big reasons people don't make plans; they fear their plans won't turn out the way they hope. I get it. I've been right there with you. But this is a very achievement-oriented, future-focused way to approach the "success" of your plans. What I've learned is that I can use a plan as a hypothesis instead of a recipe for success.

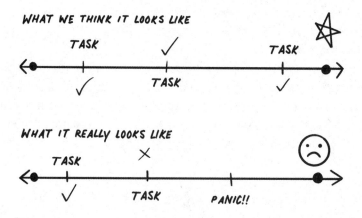

LINEAR PLANNING

WHAT WE THINK IT LOOKS LIKE

TASK   TASK

TASK

WHAT IT REALLY LOOKS LIKE

TASK

TASK   PANIC!!

When each part of my plan is a hypothesis, every action I take is an experiment. And there's no such thing as a failed experiment. The result of an experiment is neutral; you either prove out the hypothesis, or you analyze the data and adjust the hypothesis. When I started writing this book in earnest, I planned to have the first *very* rough draft done by the end of January 2022. That was my hypothesis for the project (an open loop project because after the first draft comes the second draft). As I write this chapter in its first iteration, I'm right on schedule. I should be done by the end of this week. So I've learned quite a bit during this month. I learned about how my current capacity accommodates book-writing. I learned how book-writing makes me feel. And I learned some things about writing *very* rough drafts, too. All of that I can take with me into the plan for the next project. But let's say I miss the mark, and it takes me until mid-February to finish the first draft. Then I would have a benchmark to reassess from. I can test adjustments. Would it be better to have a set word count to work toward every day? Would I benefit from attending a daily virtual writing session? Would I make more progress if I cut back even further on my other responsibilities? I could test one or two of them when I head into draft two. This is a form of reactive control, which I touch on in Chapter 7.

Another way to think about this is the process that Albert Bandura describes as a self-regulatory system. His theory is that self-regulatory systems make it easier to avoid outside influence and build a foundation for more intentional action.[92] I think this is very true—and I think that we're surrounded by the message that we can't trust our own self-regulation. Further, technology—far from simplifying our mental load—has added often unmanageable complexity to our lives and work such that we are forced to outsource regulation to apps and planners. No doubt, apps and planners are useful tools but, if they're the sole (or even the dominant) source of our motivation, we start to lose a critical relationship to what we're working on. It's impossible to utilize reactive control if you're merely checking off items on an automatically generated list without analysis or critical thinking. Bandura makes it clear that we lose influence over our own actions when we don't pay close attention to how our behavior is contributing to results. That's often exactly how we use our apps and planners, though. We list out our projects, assign deadlines to tasks, and wait for the notification that something is due. The system tells us what to work on rather than our own cognition. Having an external record of what needs to be done and when it's due is wonderful, but maintaining an active relationship to that work allows us to learn when we need to make adjustments. Without that active relationship, there cannot be a helpful feedback loop.

Feedback loop planning isn't difficult. Envision the outcome that excites you. Make a guess about what it'll take to achieve it. Take action and gather information as you go. Make adjustments. I have no doubt that there is some aspect of your life in which you already behave in this way. It might not be conscious, but it's there. Yet, if your self-efficacy is lacking, it can be a challenge to apply this kind of planning to higher stakes projects. The results are worth it, though. We don't have to learn an entirely new way of planning. We have to forget all the ways we've learned not to trust ourselves.

PLANNING AS A LEARNING PROCESS

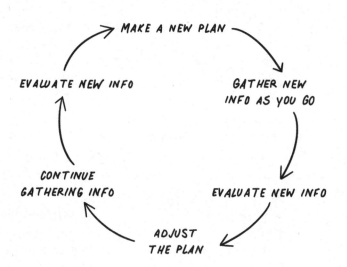

Keep it simple. To manage this process for yourself, you can use your Project Brief. Record what you expect to happen, what actually happens, and what factors might have influenced results. Then, document your adjustment or new expectation. Keep going through the cycle until the project is either complete or you decide to go in a new direction based on what you learn. If you're part of a larger team, this can be a helpful process to review with others, especially if you're more of an external processor. If you're on your own, just the process of writing things down can help immensely. If you prefer to talk things out, grab a friend for a weekly review and trade notes over coffee or email.

Following Through

I played fastpitch softball as a kid. And while I enjoyed a number of positions on the field, my favorite thing was pitching—and I was good. If you've ever seen a fastpitch softball player pitch, you've seen the comically large motion that generates the speed and play on the ball as it crosses home plate. The pitcher takes a step back with one leg as they make a small backbend to bring the ball to their chest. Then, they pull the ball back behind them with one arm, step forward, and quickly make a huge circle with their pitching arm. They release the ball at the point where their arm reaches their hip.

What you probably don't see in that exaggerated motion is the follow-through. While releasing the ball, the pitcher flicks their wrist upward allowing the ball to roll off their fingertips. This generates so much energy that their arm actually keeps going until it's back up at chest height. The follow-through generates most of the speed that a pitch has. And the way the ball rolls off of the fingertips determines whether the pitch will be a change-up, riser, or curve ball. Tiny changes to a pitcher's follow-through produce dramatic changes to how a batter experiences a pitch. I used to practice that wrist snap at the end of the pitch over and over again because, when I got the follow-through right, I was in control on the mound.

Follow-through is key to the way we approach growth and planning, too. We often make a grand production of planning (even when it doesn't include time or intention for strategy). But we rarely put the same quality of energy into the follow-through. This is not to say that you don't work hard or that you don't often find yourself working longer and more urgently than you'd like. Follow-through isn't about the *quantity* of energy you bring to a project. It's about the *quality* of that energy. It's finesse.

Your follow-through isn't measured by achieving your goal or even accomplishing a particular outcome. Your follow-through is the intent to bring the work to fruition, continually engaging the work with a curious mind to what's happening. You follow through when you pay close enough attention that you realize a project actually needs to be canceled or that you need to pivot on your plans. You don't follow through when you earnestly check things off a list or stick with plans that aren't working for the sake of discipline. Sometimes follow-through is gracefully declaring an incorrect hypothesis or a change in priorities based on thorough analysis.

Often, we let old projects live rent free in our minds (and our planners). They're projects you haven't quite let go of yet or experiments you tell yourself you'll get back to one day. Even if you try to avoid these projects or commitments, they take up a surprising amount of mental real estate. They leave dirty socks on the floor and never wash the dishes. Following through prevents this kind of mess. You regularly assess and reassess—which means you develop a habit to cull the projects that aren't serving you or your vision.

Planner, Know Thyself

If you start to notice repeating patterns that get in your way of meeting expectations (hint: you will), it's time to revisit the immunity to change framework. What competing commitments might inhibit your progress? What assumptions might make it difficult to set proper expectations for yourself? Also, take notice of any aspects of planning or creating projects that regularly trip you up. Some people are good about getting started and need help with the finishing. Others excel at finishing but have a hard time getting started. Still others trip up in the middle of projects when things don't quite go as planned.

You might notice that you have a particular trigger (or triggers) that create friction for you. I'm easily derailed by a negative email or research rabbit hole. You might get tripped up by having to enlist help or learn a new skill. When are you most likely to lose your way? Why? Once you've identified those common patterns or triggers, look for the root belief. Do you have a fear of disappointing people as I do? Do you try to maintain a certain level of comfort at all costs? Do you believe that you don't have enough skill or experience to complete the project that's important to you? Do you believe that "people like me" don't "do things like this?"

The more I excavate this self-knowledge, the more aware of it I am in the moment. When I know what my patterns have been in the past, I notice when I start leaning toward one of those patterns and redirect. I find these are the times when my commitments become particularly useful. Since part of my personal desire for growth is becoming the person I envision for my future and my commitments are based on that desire, at least one of them is usually uncannily applicable to whatever situation is tripping me up. How would the person you're becoming respond in this situation? How would they behave differently than the pattern you've developed to this point?

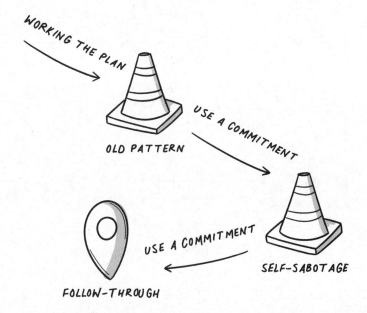

When we take a closer look at the habits that get in our way, we gain a better understanding of the ways we create our own problems. We don't learn anything when we ignore these patterns. Instead of fearing what trips us up, we can assume those patterns will play out and put a plan in place for when they do. That plan could be as simple as to ask for more time to consider next steps, remind yourself of one of your commitments, or check in with a friend who always helps you see things in a different way. When you notice yourself procrastinating, you've already made a plan to spend just 10 minutes on the task you're avoiding. When you notice yourself avoiding asking for help, you've already made a plan to reach out to someone you trust. When you notice your perfectionism kicking in, you can decide to ship something as it is! Planning for my own patterns and habits instead of hoping they just don't show their ugly faces has been a complete game-changer for me. And while I don't want to make this sound easy—because it's not—I will say that how quickly I could retrain these patterns really surprised me.

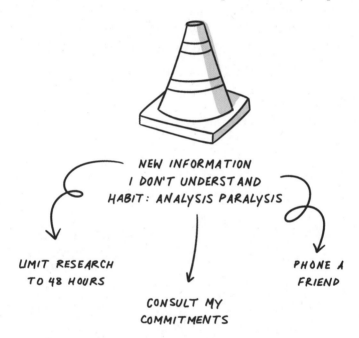

NEW INFORMATION
I DON'T UNDERSTAND
HABIT: ANALYSIS PARALYSIS

LIMIT RESEARCH
TO 48 HOURS

CONSULT MY
COMMITMENTS

PHONE A
FRIEND

Self-Sabotage and Complicit Suffering

The habits and patterns I describe here might be familiar to you as methods of self-sabotage. You might know that you often work against your own desires by procrastinating, denying help, engaging in negative self-talk, or any other form of self-sabotage. Because of the influence of rugged individualism and the doctrine of personal responsibility, you might see these behaviors as personal failings, even moral failings. But often, these behaviors are products of trauma and oppressive systems.

Why are we so likely to engage in negative self-talk when we embark on a new project? Well, one reason is that capitalist powers benefit when we are driven to consume by our bad feelings. Why deny ourselves the help we need? Rugged individualism has taught us that our success isn't our own if we're not the sole creators of it. Throughout this book, I've tried to strike a balance between personal action and agency in our own growth and acknowledging the real setbacks we face within social systems and toxic relationships. And when it comes to self-sabotage, this balance is of utmost importance.

It's neither true that we're powerless and at the mercy of others, nor that we're in complete control of our circumstances or ability to change them. Philosopher Alycia LaGuardia-LoBianco uses the term *complicit suffering* to describe the layered ways we can both be the objects of harm and disadvantage in oppressive systems, violence, or trauma and behave in ways that make this suffering worse. *Complicit suffering*, as LaGuardia-LoBianco defines it, is when we cause ourselves harm or make things harder than they have to be because our behaviors is influenced by forces outside our control. It's what happens when we internalize injustice and oppression.[93]

The concept of complicit suffering makes me think about the research on how women tend not to apply for jobs they don't feel completely qualified for, while men happily submit a subpar resume for the same job. It's easy to say that those women don't have enough confidence or lack the ambition to try, but that ignores how many times women have been told that they're *not* good enough or that they *don't* belong. I also think of all the ways that poverty is pathologized and how impoverished people are made object lessons to encourage better financial decision-making. All the while, we ignore the real external forces that exacerbate what's dubbed financially questionable behavior.

To acknowledge our complicity in suffering isn't to engage in victim-blaming, of course. Instead, it's the awareness that many of us have been on the receiving end of social injustice *and* that our action is shaped by that injustice, often making the effects worse. For instance, as an autistic person, I know that my neurology makes working in social settings exhausting. Yet, the dominant work culture of the United States is a social, extroverted one. I've been socialized to adapt myself to that culture and ignore the real pain it can cause me. I alleviate the personal and professional consequences I might suffer when I take on behavior that doesn't come naturally to me (autistic masking). That behavior then creates internal consequences. The trade-off is complicit suffering. Instead, I can restructure my work to create more flexible, asynchronous, remote opportunities. And, I can create guardrails on the amount of time I spend in social settings. As LaGuardia-LoBianco argues, that's part of my moral duty to self-care. Similarly, a person who has experienced a pattern of racist discrimination in their career might develop a pattern of negative self-talk—what's previously been described as imposter complex. They may have little power to change the systemic racism they're subject to, but by even acknowledging that their negative self-talk is an internalization of material oppression, they reclaim agency and fulfill their duty to self-care.

I really appreciate LaGuardia-LoBianco's shift from self-sabotaging behaviors to self-care behaviors, even when that shift is as simple as noticing the root cause of the self-sabotage. It's so easy to just say "I've got to stop procrastinating!" But without replacing that behavior with a different behavior, it's difficult to make a real change. When you identify the root cause of the procrastination and create a self-care behavior that helps you move through it, you can reclaim your agency. You can choose to name the behavior ("Look at that! I'm procrastinating again"), notice the underlying belief ("I'm afraid I'm not up for the task"), and acknowledge the source of that belief ("Powerful people have told me I won't be good at this because I'm a woman"). It's like in the *Harry Potter* books when Professor Lupin taught the Defense Against the Dark Arts class how to guard against "boggarts," which appear as your biggest fear. He used the "Riddikulus" charm to turn the boggart from his greatest fear into something silly and disarming. When you acknowledge that your self-sabotage has roots in oppression, trauma, loss, or the actions of others, you turn what feels like an immutable fear into something that can be, if not overcome, then mitigated.

LaGuardia-LoBianco warns that, because it can be a challenge to know whether the cause of suffering is more our responsibility or more the responsibility of outside influences, we tend toward two extremes. She writes, "Either they fail to see the forces that have shaped them to suffer, and take on full responsibility for their suffering, or see *only* these forces, and fail to see their own role in their suffering." I certainly have experiences on both sides of that spectrum. My guess is that you do too. Neither extreme is particularly useful. When we can locate ourselves somewhere in the middle of this spectrum, though, we can rediscover our power—even if there are still things we can't change.

LaGuardia-LoBianco's "duty to self-care" is not another to-do to add to the list, which is so often the case with conventional (read: co-opted) self-care advice. Instead, it's a call to reframe the situation and our relationship to it entirely. When we experience a setback in our plans or our growth, we don't have to see it as evidence that we are "hopelessly damaged." We can use these setbacks to shine a light on our limitations—current ones or persistent ones—and find a course of action that is within our control. That's empowerment. None of this is to say that it's our *sole* responsibility to care for ourselves in some Randian throwback. Instead, we acknowledge that we have a crucial role to play in our own empowerment while working with the care of others and resisting the forces that are still at work against us.

So what can we do for ourselves as we recognize our role and seek to reclaim our agency amid self-sabotage? LaGuardia-LoBianco offers a practical framework:

1. Avoid behaviors that exacerbate your suffering or put you in situations where self-sabotage is inevitable.
2. Refrain from harming yourself, including negative self-talk and self-deprecation.
3. Reach out to others and fill in your self-care gaps with care from external sources.
4. Practice noticing the sources of your self-sabotage and disempowerment.
5. Connect with others who reclaim their power and change their behavior.
6. Build an "agency emergency plan" so you know what resources you have access to shift your mood, relieve suffering, or find some peace.

Slow, gentle planning can be its own form of self-care. When we respect our capacity and honor our limits, we're better equipped to stop or avoid self-sabotage before it gets to be too much. At the same time, we have the space to notice where old conditioning might guide us more than our vision or values. Caring for ourselves, including taking our time to set targets and make plans, ensures we have the resources to flex and adapt as the need arises. I told a friend recently that a moment taken to pause and breathe is never a moment wasted. I don't know that I always heed that advice myself, but I certainly know it to be true.

Leave Room for Margin

LaGuardia-LoBianco's work references Audre Lorde, who wrote about self-care as she organized and supported a movement of Black feminists, all the while battling cancer. Lorde's declaration that caring for yourself isn't a personal indulgence, but a political act is cited often in attempts to wrest the self-care concept back from consumer capitalism and white appropriation. But there are a few sentences that precede that line that add depth to what we've explored throughout this book. Lorde writes in the epilogue to *A Burst of Light*, "Overextending myself is not stretching myself. I had to accept how difficult it is to monitor the difference."[94] Lorde had a deep desire to stretch herself in her creative work, in her organizing, in her visions for the future. But she understood that none of that was possible when she was overextended. She needed to leave room at the margins of her life in order to stretch. When she was overextended, those margins disappeared.

A few paragraphs later, Lorde continues, "I train myself for triumph knowing that it is mine, no matter what." We overextend ourselves when we question our ability to triumph, to lean into the life and work that is truly important to us. We extend ourselves beyond any measure of sustainability to prove to ourselves that we're capable—and worthy—of the triumphant life. I can't say that I possess the same confidence that Lorde has when she declares her triumph *no matter what*. I don't have the profound presence she writes about practicing. But I know that when I walk the fine line between stretching myself and overextending myself, I feel triumphant. And I know that I can return to that feeling when I've gone to far.

Lorde writes that she had to accept how difficult it is to monitor the difference between stretching and overextending. And it *is* difficult.

Yet, we can cultivate self-awareness of our capacities, our resources, to contain ourselves within a boundary that encourages exploration without creating an undeniable temptation toward overextension. I think of this boundary as margin—the empty space around a page, a park or a community, or the difference between things, like a profit margin or a margin of victory. Margin is *space*. And one thing our plans and commitments almost always lack is space. Timeframes bump up against each other, deadlines overlap, accounts lack padding. We don't leave margin between projects or items in a checklist. We certainly don't make room for error. This is a recipe for overextending ourselves. But when we leave space, we have room to stretch out, if we're so moved.

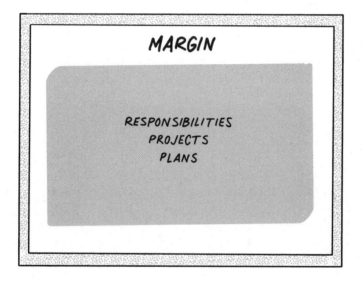

With no margin, our lives and work feel rushed, harried, and full of anxiety. We're more likely to make mistakes, and do harm to ourselves or others. With no margin, everything feels urgent. We try to tackle too many things at once. We think we can do things faster or cheaper than we really can. With no margin, it's easy to ignore our families or intimate relationships. Maybe we pull too many all-nighters or resort to choices and tactics that damage the community or industry ecosystem we're a part of. We might even start to believe the horrible things we say about ourselves; how slow we are, how unprepared we are, how unskilled we are. When we're constantly overextending ourselves to execute our plans, we open ourselves to all sorts of triggers and negative influences. We've inherited a pattern of overscheduling, overplanning, and overcommitting as well as tools (like habit trackers and to-do lists that flash a notification when we're not on top of things) that induce urgency and breed anxiety. This is no way to find joy or triumph in life, no way to do creative work or engage in critical thinking.

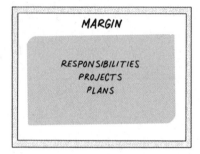

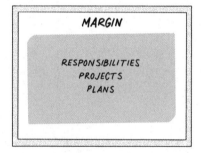

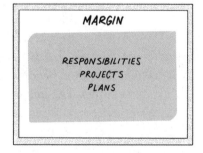

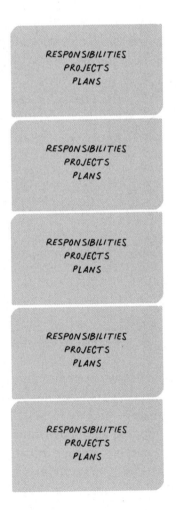

Margin is the solution. As I mention in Chapter 5, last year, I experimented with "zero-based scheduling." Zero-based scheduling allowed me to see just how little margin I gave myself, and just how much margin I really needed. It gave me a much better feel for how long certain activities take, how long I need for a lunch break, and how few things I could commit to at once. With zero-based scheduling, I could actually see my margin (or at least the optimistic hope for margin) on my calendar. And I knew when I was betraying myself by extending a project past its temporal boundary and cutting down on my margin. I haven't kept up with zero-based scheduling, but the way I structure my work day now is deeply informed by the lessons I learned during the experiment. Even if you don't want to put yourself through your own zero-based scheduling experiment, you can learn to leave more margin. Time-tracking can be helpful. Or logging your daily activities in a journal as you do them. Or simply noting how many items you're able to complete on your to-do list each day. Any method that helps you bring attention to how you use your time and either create or alleviate urgency is helpful for building margin back into your life so you can stretch out a bit more.

When you leave room for margin, you acknowledge that the time you have is valuable outside of its potential for productivity. Most of us carry with us Benjamin Franklin's old adage, "Time is money." And so, we also carry with us an assumption that time "wasted" is money wasted. The unscheduled, unfilled, unproductive time can feel like burning Benjamins. But it pays dividends with reduced stress and greater life/work satisfaction. Not only making room for margin but making that margin sacred keeps you out of The Validation Spiral. It helps you combat outside influences and harmful systems. It increases your sense of agency and capacity for self-efficacy. It gives you a better sense of your own needs and how you want to divide your resources. I believe that we can create incredible things in this life—and become extraordinary people living in extraordinary communities. The key to realizing that isn't trying to fit more in, do things faster, or navigate "the rules" better than other people. The key to this remarkable success is recognizing that what works will always take patience.

Reflection:

- What most often trips you up in planning or executing on your plans? What will you do when you experience those patterns?
- How can you build feedback loops into the projects you're planning?
- In what ways have past trauma or negative experiences influenced your behavior? What can you do to care for yourself when that behavior might derail your growth?
- How much margin are you currently working with? How could you build additional margin into your plans or schedule?

Conclusion

I LIKE TO think about big, messy, complex tasks as algebra equations. There are a whole slew of variables that I need to figure out to solve the problem. When it comes to how we set goals and plan for life or work, we tend to use our shoulds and supposed-tos as constants—values that can make the more challenging variables easier to solve for. But when shoulds and supposed-tos are constants, we conform to those factors rather than listen to our own needs or desires. As we do, we limit the ways we can solve the problem.

What happens if we use our own needs and desires as constants? What if our personal visions can help us determine the value of the variables that are most important to us? What if we decide the only way to solve the problem is to keep the commitments we've made to ourselves? Solving your personal equation this way is challenging. There are far fewer examples to learn from. And things might get even messier or more complex before the way forward comes into focus.

I have to admit that I really despise writing conclusions. I think it's because the nature of what I'm curious about will always lead to more questions than it answers, more trails of thought to meander down. I know I should write something here that wraps this all up with a bow and provides you with an inspirational send-off to go live your best life. But I don't actually believe in that as a writer or thinker. I want things to stay a little open-ended, the same way that the process I've shared leaves things a little open-ended. I welcome the mess of variables in this equation because, to me, those variables represent possibility, potential, opportunity.

From the beginning, my intention has been that, whether or not you take up the particular process I describe, you'll have new tools (and a new appreciation for) questioning your assumptions. That any "that's just the way things are" thinking becomes a Pavlovian trigger for examining what's really going on. That instead of seeking clear instructions where there are none, you experiment and systematically discover what works for you in a world that's trying to convince you that it knows better.

So What Works?

What works when it comes to our goals, plans, and visions? If you've made it this far, you know that what works is to resist shoulds and supposed-tos thrust on us by systems that weren't built with our success or the success of our communities in mind. Those shoulds and supposed-tos are the evidence of all the conditioning we're subjected to through marketing, education, political systems, and work cultures. While doing the research for this project, I came across this line from Kierkegaard's *The Lily of the Field and the Bird of the Air* (Chapter 9): "So learn, then, from the lily and the bird, learn this, the dexterity of the unconditioned."[95] I've had a sticky note with "dexterity of the unconditioned" on my iMac ever since I read that. I'm not sure if this is exactly what Kierkegaard had in mind. But what these words mean to me is that, when I shed my shoulds and supposed-tos, I realize the agility and skillfulness I can bring to any project I truly care about. I have so much to gain when I recognize my own drive beneath all the conditioning. Growth—personal and professional—is more about how I become more of myself rather than how I climb the ladder.

The thought I'd like to leave you with is this: Embrace rigor instead of rigidity. Conditioning, in all its forms, tries to squeeze us into a rigid idea of success, belonging, and productivity. The more social, economic, and political conditioning influences our goals and behavior, the better our social, economic, and political systems seem to work. But it's an illusion. Rigidity will never give us enough space to stretch out and explore our humanity. Rigor, on the other hand, requires dexterity. Rigor requires finesse. Rigor requires practice. To approach personal and professional growth with rigor is to approach it with curiosity. Rigor inspires us to unusual—and sometimes uncomfortable—questions. A rigorous life is one full of learning, delight, and openness.

I wish you the best in questioning your assumptions about what's necessary or possible and finding what works for you.

Notes

Introduction

1. Associated Press. "'The Secret' Author Rhonda Byrne's 'Greatest Secret' out in November." *USA TODAY*, 14 Aug. 2020. www .usatoday.com/story/entertainment/books/2020/08/14/the-secret-author-rhonda-byrnes-greatest-secret-out-november/3374285001/. Accessed 21 March 2022.
2. Byrne, Rhonda. *The Secret: The 10th Anniversary Edition.* New York: Atria Books, 2016.
3. Bowler, Kate. *Blessed: A History of the American Prosperity Gospel.* New York: Oxford University Press, 2018.
4. Norman Vincent Peale. *The Power of Positive Thinking and the Amazing Results of Positive Thinking.* New York: Fireside/Simon & Schuster, 2005.
5. brown, adrienne maree. *Emergent Strategy: Shaping Change, Changing Worlds.* Chico, CA: AK Press, 2017.
6. Taylor, Sonya Renee. "Brené with Sonya Renee Taylor on 'the Body Is Not an Apology.'" *Unlocking Us*, 16 Sept. 2020, brenebrown.com/ podcast/brene-with-sonya-renee-taylor-on-the-body-is-not-an-apology/. Accessed 16 Mar. 2022.

Chapter 1

7. Petersen, Anne Helen. *Can't Even: How Millennials Became the Burnout Generation*. New York: Vintage, 2022.
8. Abdulfateh, Rund, et al. "Capitalism: What Makes Us Free? *Throughline*." NPR.org, 21 July 2021, www.npr.org/2021/06/28/1011062075/capitalism-what-makes-us-free. Accessed 16 Mar. 2022.
9. Hayek, Friedrich A. "Individualism: True and False." *Individualism and Economic Order*. (Fifth Impression.). Chicago: University of Chicago Press, 1969.
10. Orgad, Shani, and Rosalind Gill. *Confidence Culture*. Durham, NC: Duke University Press, 2022.
11. Tulshyan, Ruchika, and Jodi-Ann Burey. "Stop Telling Women They Have Imposter Syndrome." *Harvard Business Review*, 11 Feb. 2021, hbr.org/2021/02/stop-telling-women-they-have-imposter-syndrome. Accessed 15 Mar. 2022.
12. Nagoski, Emily, and Amelia Nagoski. *Burnout: The Secret to Unlocking the Stress Cycle*. New York: Ballantine Books, 2020.
13. Pearson, Amy, and Kieran Rose. "A Conceptual Analysis of Autistic Masking: Understanding the Narrative of Stigma and the Illusion of Choice." *Autism in Adulthood*, vol. 3, no. 1, 22 Jan. 2021, 10.1089/aut.2020.0043.
14. Eskandani, Shirin. "EP 282: Finding Support through Coaching with Wholehearted Coaching Founder Shirin Eskandani." *What Works with Tara McMullin*, 26 May 2020, explorewhatworks.com/finding-support-through-coaching-shirin-eskandani/. Accessed 15 Mar. 2022.
15. Selassie, Sebene. *You Belong: A Call for Connection*. New York: HarperOne, 2022.

Chapter 2

16. Ehrenreich, Barbara. *Bright-Sided: How Positive Thinking Is Undermining America*. New York: Picador, 2010.
17. Rothman, Lily. "Why Bill Clinton Signed the Welfare Reform Bill, as Explained in 1996." *Time*, 16 Aug. 2016, time.com/4446348/welfare-reform-20-years/. Accessed 16 Mar. 2022.
18. Covert, Bryce. "The Myth of the Welfare Queen." *The New Republic*, 2 July 2019, nwwrepublic.com/article/154404/myth-welfare-queen. Accessed 16 Mar. 2022.
19. Fisher, Mark. *Capitalist Realism: Is There No Alternative?* Winchester, UK: Zero Books, 2009.

20. Keynes, John Maynard. "Economic Possibilities for Our Grand-children (1930)." *Essays in Persuasion*, by John Maynard Keynes, New York: Harcourt Brace, 1932.

21. Fraser, Nancy, and Bhaskar Sunkara. *The Old Is Dying and the New Cannot Be Born: From Progressive Neoliberalism to Trump and Beyond.* London, New York: Verso, 2019.

22. Monbiot, George. "Neoliberalism—The Ideology at the Root of All Our Problems." *The Guardian*, 29 Nov. 2016, www.theguardian.com/books/2016/apr/15/neoliberalism-ideology-problem-george-monbiot. Accessed 16 Mar. 2022.

23. Hayek, Friedrich A. "Individualism: True and False." *Individualism and Economic Order*. (Fifth Impression.). Chicago: University of Chicago Press, 1969.

24. Hoover, Herbert, and University of Virginia Miller Center. "October 22, 1928: Principles and Ideals of the United States Government | Miller Center." *Millercenter.org*, University of Virginia, 20 Oct. 2016, millercenter.org/the-presidency/presidential-speeches/october-22-1928-principles-and-ideals-united-states-government. Accessed 16 May 2022.

25. Weber, Max, and Talcott Parsons. *The Protestant Ethic and the Spirit of Capitalism*. Kettering, OH: Angelico Press, 2014.

26. Okun, Tema. "Characteristics." *White Supremacy Culture*, May 2021, www.whitesupremacyculture.info/characteristics.html. Accessed 21 Mar. 2022.

27. Taylor, Sonya Renee. "Brené with Sonya Renee Taylor on 'the Body Is Not an Apology.'" *Unlocking Us*, 16 Sept. 2020, brenebrown.com/podcast/brene-with-sonya-renee-taylor-on-the-body-is-not-an-apology/. Accessed 16 Mar. 2022.

28. Seven, Zuva. "Success Garnered from Self-Erasure Isn't Something I Want." *Medium*, 23 Dec. 2019, aninjusticemag.com/success-garnered-from-self-erasure-isnt-something-i-want-79839ae69a0. Accessed 7 Apr. 2022.

29. Joyner, Lisa. "Top 10 New Year's Resolutions for 2022 Revealed." *unlocki*, 3 Jan. 2022, www.countryliving.com/uk/news/a38576418/new-years-resolutions-2022/. Accessed 16 Mar. 2022.

Chapter 3

30. Biss, Eula. *Having and Being Had*. London: Faber and Faber, 2022.

31. Glei, Jocelyn K. "Jocelyn K. Glei—Who Are You without the Doing?" *Hurry Slowly*, 6 Nov. 2018, hurryslowly.co/203-jocelyn-k-glei/. Accessed 17 Mar. 2022.

32. Wallace, Kathleen. "The Self Is Not Singular but a Fluid Network of Identities/Aeon Essays." *Aeon*, 18 May 2021, aeon.co/essays/the-self-is-not-singular-but-a-fluid-network-of-identities. Accessed 17 Mar. 2022.

33. Verhaeghe, Paul, and Jane Hedley-Prôle. *What about Me? The Struggle for Identity in a Market-Based Society*. Brunswick, Victoria: Scribe Publications, 2014.

34. Tolentino, Jia. *Trick Mirror: Reflections on Self-Delusion*. New York: 4th Estate, 2019.

35. Seymour, Richard. *Twittering Machine*. London: Verso, 2020.

36. Nonfiction Research, and Bodacious Strategy Studio. "From Dependence to Independence: The Rise of the Independent Creator." 2022. Commissioned by Mighty Networks.

37. Jennings, Rebecca. "The Influencers Are Burned Out, Too." *Vox*, 25 May 2021, www.vox.com/the-goods/2021/5/25/22451987/influencer-burnout-tiktok-clubhouse. Accessed 17 Mar. 2022.

38. Kegan, Robert. *The Evolving Self: Problem and Process in Human Development*. Cambridge: Harvard University Press London, 2001.

39. Petersen, Anne Helen, and Charlie Warzel. "How to Care Less about Work." *The Atlantic*, 5 Dec. 2021, www.theatlantic.com/ideas/archive/2021/12/how-care-less-about-work/620902/. Accessed 21 Mar. 2022.

Chapter 4

40. Attenberg, Jami. *I Came All This Way to Meet You: Writing Myself Home*. New York: Ecco, An Imprint of Harpercollins Publishers, 2022.

41. Setiya, Kieran. *Midlife: A Philosophical Guide*. Princeton, NJ: Princeton University Press, 2018.

42. Salzberg, Sharon. *Real Change: Mindfulness to Heal Ourselves and the World*. New York: Flatiron Books, 2021.

43. Meadows, Donella, and The Donella Meadows Project. "Dancing with Systems." *The Academy for Systems Change*, donellameadows.org/archives/dancing-with-systems/. Accessed 21 Mar. 2022.

44. Roth, Bernard. *The Achievement Habit: Stop Wishing, Start Doing, and Take Command of Your Life*. New York: Harper Business, An Imprint of HarperCollins Publishers, 2015.

45. Hollis, Rachel. *Girl, Wash Your Face: Stop Believing the Lies about Who You Are so You Can Become Who You Were Meant to Be*. Nashville: Nelson Books, 2020.

46. Grady, Constance. "Why the Author of Girl, Stop Apologizing Had to Apologize Twice in a Week." *Vox*, 9 Apr. 2021, www.vox.com/culture/22373865/rachel-hollis-controversy-harriet-tubman-girl-wash-your-face-stop-apologizing-unrelatable. Accessed 21 Mar. 2022.

47. Tracy, Brian. *Goals!* San Francisco, CA: Berrett-Koehler; Maidenhead, 2003.

48. Traister, Rebecca. *Good and Mad: The Revolutionary Power of Women's Anger*. New York: Simon & Schuster, 2019.

49. Brickman, Phillip, and Donald T. Campbell. "Hedonic Relativism and Planning the Good Society." *Adaptation Level Theory: A Symposium, New York*, edited by M. H. Apley. New York: Academic Press, 1971, pp. 287–302.

50. Alderson, Arthur S., and Tally Katz-Gerro. "Compared to Whom? Inequality, Social Comparison, and Happiness in the United States." *Social Forces*, vol. 95, no. 1, 6 June 2016, pp. 25–54, 10.1093/sf/sow042. Accessed 13 Jan. 2022.

51. brown, adrienne maree. "Build as We Fight: Remarks from the 2019 American Studies Association Annual Meeting—Adrienne Maree Brown." *Adrienne Maree Brown*, 10 Nov. 2019, adriennemareebrown.net/2019/11/10/build-as-we-fight-remarks-from-the-2019-american-studies-association-annual-meeting/. Accessed 21 Mar. 2022.

52. Orgad and Gill. *Confidence Culture*.

Chapter 5

53. Lawson, Jenny. *Broken (in the Best Possible Way)*. New York: Henry Holt and Company, 2021.

54. Tate, Amethyst. "Beyonce and Jay Z Reportedly Give $6.4 Million in Bonuses to Employees." *International Business Times*, 7 Aug. 2013, www.ibtimes.com/beyonce-jay-z-reportedly-give-64-million-bonuses-employees-1375397. Accessed 17 May 2022.

55. Adam, Barbara. "When Time Is Money: Contested Rationalities of Time and Challenges to the Theory and Practice of Work." *Orca.cardiff.ac.uk*, 1 Oct. 2001, orca.cardiff.ac.uk/id/eprint/78053. Accessed 21 Mar. 2022.

56. Jackson, Elisabeth. "How Do You Measure Quality Time?" *What Works*, 22 Feb. 2022, explorewhatworks.com/how-do-you-measure-quality-time-with-elisabeth-jackson-time-money-3/.

57. Miserandino, Christine. "The Spoon Theory Written by Christine Miserandino—But You Don't Look Sick? Support for Those with Invisible Illness or Chronic Illness." *But You Don't Look Sick? Support for Those with Invisible Illness or Chronic Illness*, 26 Apr. 2013, butyoudontlooksick.com/articles/written-by-christine/the-spoon-theory/.

58. Taylor, Sonya Renee. *The Body Is Not an Apology: The Power of Radical Self-Love*. Oakland, CA: Berrett-Koehler Publishers, 2018.

59. Brittany, Berger. "Updating Your Default Settings." *What Works*, 2021, explorewhatworks.com/updating-your-default-settings-brittany-berger/.

60. Standing, Guy. *The Precariat: The New Dangerous Class*. London, New York: Bloomsbury, 2014.

61. Petersen. *Can't Even*.

62. Hochschild, Arlie Russell. *The Managed Heart: Commercialization of Human Feeling*. Ann Arbor, MI: Umi, 1983.

Chapter 6

63. O'Rourke, Meghan. *The Invisible Kingdom: Reimagining Chronic Illness*. New York: Riverhead Books, 2022.

64. Barry, Rita. "What Does Growth without Striving Look Like?" *What Works*, 11 Jan. 2022, explorewhatworks.com/what-does-growth-without-striving-look-like-rita-barry/.

65. Hollis. *Girl, Wash Your Face*.

66. Nguyen, C. Thi. *Games: Agency as Art*. New York: Oxford University Press, 2020.

67. Locke, Edwin A., and Gary P. Latham. *A Theory of Goal Setting & Task Performance*. Englewood Cliffs, NJ: Prentice Hall, 1990.

68. Nguyen, C. Thi (2021). "How Twitter Gamifies Communication." In Jennifer Lackey (ed.), *Applied Epistemology*. Oxford: Oxford University Press. pp. 410–436.

69. Glatzel, Mara. "Building a Business Based on What Matters." *What Works*, 5 Oct. 2021, explorewhatworks.com/building-a-business-based-on-what-matters-mara-glatzel/.

70. Bandura, Albert. "Self Efficacy | Psychologist | Social Psychology | Stanford University | California." *Albertbandura.com*, 2012, albertbandura.com/albert-bandura-self-efficacy.html. Accessed 17 May 2022.

71. Avenir, Sarah. "Leading through Uncertainty." *What Works*, 14 July 2020, explorewhatworks.com/leading-through-uncertainty-sarah-avenir/.

Chapter 7

72. Covert, Abby. *How to Make Sense of Any Mess*. Abby Covert, 2014.
73. Bandura, Albert. "Social Cognitive Theory of Self-Regulation." *Organizational Behavior and Human Decision Processes*, vol. 50, no. 2, Dec. 1991, pp. 248–287, 10.1016/0749-5978(91)90022-l.
74. Pink, Daniel H. *Drive*. New York: Riverhead Books, 2009.
75. Nguyen, "How Twitter Gamifies Communication."
76. Selassie, Sebene. "The Delusion of Separation." *Hurry Slowly*, 11 Aug. 2020, hurryslowly.co/312-sebene-selassie/.
77. Maslow, Abraham. "A Theory of Human Motivation." *Psychological Review*, vol. 50, no. 4, 1943, doi.apa.org/doiLanding?doi=10.1037%2Fh0054346.

Chapter 8

78. De Beauvoir, Simone. *The Ethics of Ambiguity*. New York: Open Road Integrated Media, 1947.
79. Kegan, Robert, and Lisa Lahey. "The Real Reason People Won't Change." *Harvard Business Review*, 10 Nov. 2015, hbr.org/2001/11/the-real-reason-people-wont-change. Accessed 29 Mar. 2022.
80. brown. *Emergent Strategy*.

Chapter 9

81. Nelson, Maggie. *On Freedom: Four Songs of Care and Constraint*. Toronto: Mcclelland & Stewart, 2021.
82. Adam, Barbara. "When Time Is Money: Contested Rationalities of Time and Challenges to the Theory and Practice of Work."
83. Selassie. *You Belong: A Call for Connection*.
84. Weber. *Protestant Ethic and the Spirit of Capitalism*.
85. Kierkegaard, Søren, and Bruce H Kirmmse. *The Lily of the Field and the Bird of the Air: Three Godly Discourses*. Princeton, Oxford: Princeton University Press, 2018.
86. Didion, Joan. *Let Me Tell You What I Mean*. New York: 4th Estate, 2022.

87. Setiya. *Midlife: A Philosophical Guide.*
88. Moran, Brian, and Michael Lennington. *Uncommon Accountability: A Radical New Approach to Greater Success and Fulfillment.* Hoboken, NJ: John Wiley & Sons, 2022.

Chapter 10

89. Montell, Amanda. *Cultish: The Language of Fanaticism.* New York: HarperCollins Publishers, 2021.
90. Gilkey, Charlie. *Start Finishing: How to Go from Idea to Done.* Louisville, CO: Publishing Sounds True, 2022.

Chapter 11

91. Ahmed, Sara. *Living a Feminist Life.* Durham, NC: Duke University Press, 2017.
92. Bandura, Albert. "Social Cognitive Theory of Self-Regulation."
93. LaGuardia-LoBianco, Alycia W. "Complicit Suffering and the Duty to Self-Care." *Philosophy*, vol. 93, no. 2, Apr. 2018, pp. 251–277, 10.1017/s0031819118000086. Accessed 19 July 2020.
94. Lorde, Audre. *A Burst of Light: And Other Essays.* Mineola, NY: Ixia Press, 2017.

Conclusion

95. Kierkegaard. *The Lily of the Field and the Bird of the Air: Three Godly Discourses.*

Acknowledgments

Thank you to Sean for being my catalyst. You have inspired me to be as curious about how I live as I am about religion, business, economics, and politics.

Thank you to Jessica Faust, my agent. You stuck with me through years of *not* committing to a book and then gracefully nurtured this idea into its current form.

Thank you to my editor, Julie, for shaping this work. And thanks to Brian and the whole team at Wiley for taking a chance on me and this message.

Thank you to Rita for the question that helped to inspire this book. And to Kate for encouraging me to explore the personal, political, and philosophical ripple effects of my values.

Thank you to the customers, clients, followers, and members who have been partners with me in figuring out this stuff. Your questions, concerns, and stories are the scaffolding upon which these ideas are built. And thanks to all of my podcast guests over the years. You've taught me to think differently about the world.

Thanks to Shannon, Kristen, Meighan, Lou, Marty, and Emily for creating the stability I needed to devote time and mental bandwidth to this project.

Thanks to Brigitte, Michael, Elizabeth, Charlie, Emily, Kathleen, and all the other incredible people who believe in me enough that I'm learning to believe in myself.

About the Author

Tara McMullin is a writer, podcaster, and producer. For over 13 years, she's studied small business owners—how they live, how they work, what influences them, and what they hope for the future. She's the host of *What Works*, a podcast about navigating the 21st-century economy with your humanity intact. Tara is also co-founder, with her husband Sean, of Yellow House Media, a boutique podcast production company. Her work has been featured in *Fast Company*, *The Startup*, *Forbes*, and *The Muse*. She lives in Lancaster County, Pennsylvania, with her husband, daughter, and two lovable cats that showed up in the backyard one day. Her heart is always in the mountains of Montana.

Index

203